PROMOTE YOUR BOOK

Other Books by Patricia Fry

Writing and Publishing Books

Publish Your Book: Proven Strategies and Resources for Enterprising Authors

How to Write a Successful Book Proposal in 8 Days or Less

The Successful Author's Handbook (e-book)

The Successful Writer's Handbook

The Author's Repair Kit: Heal Your Publishing Mistakes and Breathe New Life Into Your Book (e-book)

A Writer's Guide to Magazine Articles

Books Just For Fun

Catscapades: True Cat Tales

Quest For Truth: A Journey of the Soul (a memoir)

PROMOTE YOUR BOOK

Over 250 Proven, Low-Cost Tips
and Techniques for the Enterprising Author

PATRICIA FRY

ALLWORTH PRESS
NEW YORK

Allworth Press books may be purchased in bulk at special discounts for sales promotion, corporate gifts, fund-raising, or educational purposes. Special editions can also be created to specifications. For details, contact the Special Sales Department, Allworth Press, 307 West 36th Street, 11th Floor, New York, NY 10018 or info@skyhorsepublishing.com.

15 14 13 12 11 5 4 3 2 1

Published by Allworth Press,
an imprint of Skyhorse Publishing, Inc.
307 West 36th Street, 11th Floor, New York, NY 10018.

Allworth Press® is a registered trademark of Skyhorse Publishing, Inc.®, a Delaware corporation.   .

www.allworth.com

ISBN: 978-1-58115-857-1

Library of Congress Cataloging-in-Publication Data

Fry, Patricia L., 1940-
Promote your book : over 250 proven, low-cost tips and techniques for the enterprising author / Patricia Fry.
    p. cm.
Includes bibliographical references and index.
ISBN 978-1-58115-857-1 (pbk.)
1. Books—United States—Marketing. 2. Authorship—Marketing. I. Title.
Z285.6.F79 2011
002.068'8—dc23
                2011016521

Printed in the United States of America.

CONTENTS

FOREWORD

Most of us, when we decide to write our first book, expect a best seller or at least one that will attract thousands upon thousands of readers on merit alone. You might envision yourself being greeted by enormous crowds at book signings throughout the country and being interviewed by this nation's top TV show hosts. You dream of launching the book and, within a few months, when sales are in the millions, stepping out of the limelight and going to work writing your next book.

What you'll soon discover is that, in order to sell even a few copies of your book, you'll have to pay at least as much attention to promoting it as you did to writing it. If you want sales to continue beyond those initial ones to family, friends, and folks who read the nice article about you in the local newspaper, you will have to keep up your promotional efforts. If you want to reach potential buyers in a wide range of arenas, you may have to market outside of your comfort zone. Any author will tell you that successful marketing takes creativity and an enterprising outlook. And this is true whether you land a traditional royalty publisher, you self-publish (establish your own publishing company), or you decide to go with one of the many hybrid pay-to-publish (vanity) services.

I have over thirty-five years experience marketing my own self-published and traditionally published books. I consult with clients on issues of book promotion. I teach an online book promotion course. And I write a monthly newsletter that focuses on book promotion for the member area of the SPAWN website. Consequently, I continue to engage in an enormous amount of research related to book promotion. In addition, through my affiliation with SPAWN (Small Publishers, Artists and Writers Network) and my participation in numerous writers' conferences, I've come to know many authors, and some of them have shared their marketing tips with me. This book is a compilation of mostly low- and no-cost book promotion ideas.

The best way to use this book is to read it from cover to cover—get a clear sense of what the process of book promotion entails and the multitude of options at your disposal. Then go back and choose those activities that resonate with you—that make sense in light of your energy, time element, skills, talents, strengths, interests, comfort level, and the topic/genre of your book.

Create an ABC list of book promotion activities. Choose those that you can most effectively weave into your own book promotion program. And then start stretching.

Maybe your A list consists of building a website, creating a blog, and promoting your book online through social media sites and through a few news release services. Once you've pursued these activities for a while, add some from your B list. Now, perhaps you're ready to start submitting articles/stories to magazines and newsletters, soliciting book reviews, and approaching the library market and a variety of specialty markets related to your book's genre/theme. This may also be a good time to amp up your blog and social media presence through the various available programs and options.

Once you have a good flow going with these activities, get really adventurous and move on to your C list. This might include giving live presentations, having a book trailer made, and doing podcasts.

By trial and error, you'll learn what works and what doesn't. If you do well at book festivals, sign up for more of them. Maybe you're selling a lot of books when you give live presentations. Consider applying for these opportunities all throughout the states. If you're becoming known as an expert in your field, begin a consulting service and add credibility to your repertoire by launching a newsletter related to your topic or genre.

Keep this book handy. You'll need it now and for the long term, for successful book promotion is not a one-time event. It is ongoing for as long as you want your book to sell.

Book Promotion Basics

The glorious moment has arrived. You've just completed your first (or twenty-first) book. It doesn't matter how many books have gone before this one, they're each your masterwork—a thrilling accomplishment.

Creating a book is not unlike creating life. The author conceives the idea, grows it inside of him/herself, and, after many months of labor, gives birth. If you doubt your emotional connection to your book, think about how difficult it was to send your "child" off to the publisher or printer. If you're like many authors, you experienced a strange sense of loss as you relinquished temporary control of your project. And you couldn't wait to hold the finished book in your hands.

Before welcoming your completed book home—in fact, even before writing it—you need to think about its future. The point of producing a book is presumably so that it will be read. At the very least, you hope to recoup your expenses. And you would not be human if you didn't dream of it bringing you fame and fortune. This won't happen, however, without your concentrated effort. It's up to you to promote your book. And the time to plan your marketing strategy is even prior to writing your first chapter.

Before starting that book, answer these questions:

- Why do I want to write this book? What is my primary reason for writing it?
- What is the point/purpose of the book?

If you're writing this book because you want to become famous, earn a lot of money, show off, prove something to someone else or yourself, you may be writing it for all of the wrong reasons. If, on the other hand, you love to write, you know you have something of value to share with a segment of people, your book will fill a definite need, and/or you want to use the book to position yourself as an expert in your field, your reasons might be valid.

When considering the purpose of your book, if you determine that you're writing it in order to change minds, make an unpopular point, or to tell the world your rather ordinary story, the validity of this book is questionable. If your purpose is to educate or inform a particular audience on a topic of interest to them or entertain readers through good writing, perhaps you're on the right track. Make sure that your reason and purpose are genuine and not frivolous.

Even when yours is a valid book with a true and significant target audience, you must understand that there's more to selling books than having them placed on the shelves in mega bookstores. In fact, it's almost impossible for a self-published author (one who has established his/her own publishing company) or a pay-to-publish author to convince major booksellers to carry their books nationwide. Managers of chain bookstores will generally special order copies of your book for customers who request it, as long as you've taken the steps necessary to be included in the main bookseller databases. And some of these stores will carry books by local authors. In order to have your book stocked in bookstores nationwide, you'll need one of two things—the support of a major traditional royalty publisher or an aggressive marketing plan that's bringing hundreds of customers into those stores asking for your book.

If your book has been published and is being distributed by a recognized traditional publisher, the chain bookstores will most likely take it on. But if sales don't meet their expectations, your book will be rotated out of stock and sent back to the publisher along with truckloads of other stagnating books.

The point is that your book won't sell itself. Its success depends on your ability and willingness to promote it, and this is true whether you have landed a traditional royalty publisher, you've self-published (established your own publishing company), or you have gone with a pay-to-publish (vanity) service. As I said, even before you put pen to paper, it's important to think realistically about marketing. And having a New York publisher doesn't change this fact.

It's hard work to promote a book. If you're still reeling from years of banging your head against the computer while writing this book and months of dealing with cover designers, editors, illustrators, printers, the bar code folks, the copyright office, etc., you ain't seen nothing yet. Published authors will tell you that producing the book is easy compared to marketing it. Publishing guides typically warn budding authors to prepare themselves for the work they'll encounter after their book is published. And yes, marketing *is* the responsibility of the author.

Remember that success doesn't usually come without some expenditure and sacrifice. Like country singing star Willie Nelson says, when asked what it was like to become an overnight success, "Being an overnight success feels pretty good considering I put in twenty years of hard work to get here."

Even before starting your book, decide whether or not you're cut out for the work ahead. As you know, writing is a relatively quiet activity—one that even an introvert can pursue successfully. But publishing and marketing are active businesses that take imagination, assertiveness, courage, persistence, and lots of energy. Not everyone is suited to do both the writing and aggressive (or even assertive) marketing. Are you?

Further, with the advent of the Internet and the obvious race to create new technology at a faster and faster pace, it is important that you learn about the marketing tools available through social media and through your own website. The technological learning curve can be difficult for someone who is not all that familiar with the digital movement. But it is oh so important if you want to participate on a level playing field.

Consider the following: time is a major factor in book promotion. The ideal would be to devote all of your waking hours to marketing your book. If you can't give the book your undivided attention, at least commit to a promotional schedule. Vow to make three contacts related to book promotion per day or spend one or two days per week pursuing marketing efforts.

And this should not be considered a temporary schedule. Don't assume that one book tour will launch your book or that one review is all you need to keep your book selling. It's likely that when you stop promoting your book, sales will dwindle and then stop.

Do you have something worthwhile to market? This is an extremely difficult question to answer. Even experienced publishers wrestle with this question, as is evidenced by some of the books they turn down that later become bestsellers and some of the losers they take on.

Why does a book fail to sell? Sometimes the timing is off—the subject has been overworked or its time has not yet come. Maybe the author hasn't hit upon the right slant for his book or the right market or marketing technique. That's why it is imperative that you research the market for your book even before you start writing it. And a book proposal can help you do this.

As we've established, marketing a book takes time, commitment, energy, and creativity. Following are additional ideas to help you launch your successful promotional program. If you select the right activities for you and your book and you proceed in an organized, methodical, diligent, and persistent manner, you will most likely succeed in your promotional efforts.

Things You Must Do Before Your Book Is a Book

Writing is only part of the process of preparing a book for publication. You must also pave the road for that book in order to eventually reach your proposed readership. Following are steps you can take to more adequately groom yourself and your book for a successful publishing experience.

Study the Publishing Industry

There are two basic steps to successful publishing. Number one is study the publishing industry. I advise authors to come out of their writing rooms often to see what's going on aboveground. What you learn about the publishing industry can, in many instances, affect the planned direction of your book. I know one author who had high aspirations of being interviewed on Oprah's show once her memoir was published. The fact that she followed my advice and spent time each week studying the publishing industry may have contributed to her potential future success. She was shocked to read in one of her publishing newsletters that Oprah was no longer reviewing memoirs. Because this author was so attached to the idea of an interview with Oprah, this caused her to rethink her book. (This occurred before Oprah announced that she was retiring.) At the time, the star was still reviewing novels and some self-help books. So this author changed the whole scope of her project to conform to the type of books Oprah was reviewing.

This is just one of many reasons why it is important to study the publishing industry before getting involved. What do you need to know about publishing? Basically, you need to know how the industry operates, what your options are, the possible consequences of your choices, and your responsibilities as a published author. You should understand how books are produced, distribution methods, and the whole world of book marketing both on- and offline.

Think of it this way, you wouldn't start any other type of business without knowing something about the way the industry works, the products, the suppliers, the distributors, the competition, and the customers. Whether you want to believe it or not, publishing is a serious business; and it is in a period of constant flux. So it is even more important than ever to keep your finger on the pulse of this industry.

How does one study the publishing industry?

- Read books by experts. I recommend my own books, as well as those by Penny Sansevieri, Steve Weber, Brian Jud, Dan Poynter, and Mark Levine.
- Read newsletters and magazines specific to authors and publishers. See my recommendations under "Resources" at my website: *www.matilijapress.com/forwriters/resources.html.*
- Join organizations such as SPAWN (Small Publishers, Artists and Writers Network), IBPA (Independent Book Publishers Association), and SPAN (Small Publishers Association of North America) and read the materials they provide.
- Attend conferences and sit in on workshops conducted by publishing professionals.
- Listen in on webinars, teleseminars, and podcasts presented by industry experts.
- Consult with one or more publishing professionals.
- Launch a study of Internet marketing techniques, software, and other options so you'll be prepared to participate in the competitive bookselling marketplace.

The second step to a successful publishing experience is to write a book proposal.

Write a Book Proposal

Some of you have already discovered that writing is a craft—it is a heart thing—and publishing, in stark contrast, is a business. Publishing is not an extension of your writing.

What is the first thing a potential entrepreneur really should do before opening his/her store, factory, or other business? Write a business plan. And that's what I (and other publishing professionals) recommend that you do—write a business plan for your book (a book proposal).

Wait—I realize that some of you have already completed a book and you're ready to start the promotional process or kick it up a notch. If, however, your book isn't doing well in the marketplace and you don't know why, consider writing an after-publication book proposal. Learn how by reading my one-of-a-kind e-book: *The Author's Repair Kit* (Matilija Press). What most struggling authors discover is that they are promoting to the wrong audience.

Whether you've finished writing your book or not, I recommend that you continue reading this section. A well-researched, well-organized book proposal will tell you whether you have a book at all, who your target audience is, and where they are. You'll discover if there is a market for your book, and you'll learn volumes about how to cultivate or develop some of your skills and how to use them in the marketing process.

You may not know this yet, but the right answer to the question, "Who is my target audience" is *not* "everyone." Through the process of writing a book proposal, you'll pinpoint your target audience. And you'll discover exactly where to find them and how to best approach them.

A book proposal typically includes a synopsis or overview (if you can't succinctly describe your proposed book, it may not be a valid project); a market analysis to determine whether your book is needed and how it compares with those currently offered; your promotional platform, ideas, connections, and skills; and a detailed chapter outline (which, by the way, will make writing the book a slam dunk).

It's tricky to second-guess the public. Even large publishing company executives have trouble predicting the market. Through a book proposal, however, you can more accurately assess the potential market for your particular book and your promotional aptitude before your book is a book. What you learn from the process of writing a book proposal could mean the difference between your publishing success and certain failure.

Let these resources help you to write a book proposal:

Write the Perfect Book Proposal by Jeff and Deborah Herman

How to Write a Successful Book Proposal by Patricia Fry

Loree Griffin Burns shares her love and knowledge of science with children through two published books—*Tracking Trash: Flotsam, Jetsam, and the Science of Ocean Movement* and *The Hive Detectives: Chronicle of a Honey Bee Catastrophe* (Houghton Mifflin).

I had the pleasure of working with Burns on her first book proposal. She recalls that, through the process, she learned that she hadn't accurately defined the book, yet. "I had to decide, was the book about a man and his work related to ocean currents or the ocean and how it moves?" As she further refined her proposal, the answer became obvious: "My book wasn't about the oceanographer, Dr. Ebbesmeyer, and his findings, but about the incredible amount of debris that floats in our oceans."

According to Burns, "I often equate writing a nonfiction book with doing a jigsaw puzzle. Writing the proposal is a lot like piecing together the four outer edges. It gives me structure, identifies boundaries, provides crucial clues as to how I should arrange the pieces inside. Once I have the edges in line, I can begin the exciting work of creating a picture out of the many, many pieces of the puzzle I have collected."

Burns adds, "I'd strongly suggest to anyone with a book idea that they develop a book proposal. Doing so requires a writer to clearly define their book idea and also to identify the structure through which they will execute it. For me, this is an extremely important part of the creative process."

Compile an Extensive Mailing/E-mailing List

I know, I know, you prefer seeing your book exhibited at mega bookstores nationwide in the center aisle. We all do. But don't get so caught up in your lofty dreams that you neglect the obvious sales—those to friends, family, acquaintances, and colleagues.

When should you start creating a mailing/e-mailing list? The moment you decide to write a book. If, however, your book has already been published, start now! It's never too late. Compile a mailing list and an e-mailing list from your personal address books, Rolodex, club rosters, and Christmas card list. Request a printout of former classmates from your high school class reunion committee. Add neighbors, former neighbors, coworkers, business associates, your insurance agent, hairdresser, children's teachers, and the owner of the gym where you work out.

Collect business cards wherever you go. Keep a running list of those who helped with the research for or the compilation of this book as well as those who have purchased any of your other books or used your services over the years. You'll find out, through this process, how important it is to keep good records.

Spend evenings pouring over the Yellow Pages locally and online. List professionals who might be interested in the topic of your book, such as psychologists, small business owners, beauticians, massage therapists, realtors, accountants, and so forth. Expand your mailing/ e-mailing list by adding the names of anyone you talk to in person or online with regard to your book project.

An author's mailing list is never finished. Keep adding to yours because you will use it over and over.

When I complete one of my local history books, I generally send announcements to my personal mailing and e-mail lists, as well as to local school administrators, educators, museum directors, librarians, the director of the chamber of commerce, city hall personnel, and the people who shared their stories with me, for example.

While marketing *The Mainland Luau: How to Capture the Flavor of Hawaii in Your Own Backyard,* my mailing list included caterers, hog farmers, the owners of meat processing companies, barbecue manufacturers, groups, and individuals who promote barbecue contests, people who collect Hawaiiana, and civic association leaders, because they sometimes present luaus as fund-raisers.

(Learn how to do mass e-mailings in chapter three.)

Purchase Mailing Lists

You can purchase mailing lists reflecting practically any classification imaginable, from religious bookstore owners to computer programmers, from senior citizens to seniors in high school. There are lists that target consumers who live in a particular region, who earn a certain income, who purchase specific products, and who have a particular hobby or interest, for example. It used to be that these lists typically came in the form of ready-to-use mailing labels. Many of them are now sent via e-mail and, in fact, may contain only e-mail addresses. There are some companies that will download e-mail addresses to your computer. Make sure you know what you're getting. The costs vary widely from company to company, so I suggest that you shop around.

Following are few websites where you can purchase mailing lists:

www.usadata.com
www.leadsplease.com
www.goleads.com
www.infousa.com
http://lists.nextmark.com
www.1000lists.com

Locate additional mailing list companies and directories by doing a Google search using keywords: "mailing lists" or "mailing list directory," or refine your search by trying "mailing list + horse owners," "mailing list + boaters," "mailing list + ecologists."

Tip: Test a list from an unknown company before purchasing others. Some mailing lists aren't maintained as well as others, and many of the addresses may be outdated.

Make Your Book More Salable

Several years ago, a gentleman came to me asking for help marketing his self-published book. He complained that bookstores wouldn't carry it, and he wondered why. As soon as I saw the book, I knew the reason. He neglected to follow any sort of self-publishing guidelines. In fact, he hadn't even bothered to find out what they are.

He did not have an ISBN (International Standard Book Number)— a system used to identify the book and the publisher. He didn't have a barcode. Most retail stores, even then, didn't stock books without barcodes. He didn't know the importance of getting listed in *Books in Print* (the database that booksellers, librarians, and others use to order books), but his book probably wouldn't have qualified anyway without an ISBN. And it would not be accepted at Amazon.com.

Another common mistake first-time publishers make is choosing an inappropriate binding for the outlets they want to pursue. Booksellers and librarians usually follow certain criteria for selecting books, and that may exclude books without spines, such as saddle-stitched books or those bound using plastic or wire spirals.

If you want to sell many or even a few copies of your book, it's imperative that you conform to certain industry standards. Study books on self-publishing such as Dan Poynters' *Self-Publishing Manual* and my book, *Publish Your Book: Proven Strategies and Resources for Enterprising Authors*.

Create a Powerful First Impression

You've heard the clichés, "Don't judge a book by its cover," and "Beauty is only skin deep." But these wise words don't exactly apply to a book. People *do* judge a book by its cover, so you must have one that will attract your audience. While it certainly is important that your message or story be well written, interesting, informative, and/or entertaining, you'll be hard-pressed to get anyone to open your book if it is unattractive.

This is not just a theory, folks. Booksellers know this to be fact. And I'm one of many who have observed the level of consumer interest in books at large book festivals. Potential customers gravitate toward books that are appealing and those that stand out from the rest while books with drab, muddy covers are repeatedly ignored.

There are a couple of areas where money should be spent when it comes to producing a book. And an important one is on the book cover. Hire a good cover designer. How do you find one? Visit book designers' / graphic artists' sites and look at their work. Get recommendations from other authors who have experienced success with their books. Here are a couple of directories of book cover designers:

www.guru.com

www.onlinedesignerdirectory.com

Build Promotion into Your Book

One excellent reason for writing a book proposal before you write (or at least before you complete) your fiction or nonfiction book is to give yourself the opportunity to build promotional hooks into your book. What do I mean by this? Your book has a target audience. It may also have one or two peripheral audiences. But you can widen your audience base by including certain elements.

For example, let's say that you're writing a book for women who read romance novels. This is a strong audience base. But you might create a larger audience if you give one of your characters a motorcycle, a horse, a pilot's license, a brain injury, or diabetes. Not only would you, perhaps, attract additional readers, but you'll also open up your promotional opportunities. If you portray the diabetic character in a positive way, the American Diabetes Association might be interested in helping you promote your book. If one of your significant characters is a woman pilot, you can also promote to aviators worldwide. If she flies stunt planes, this opens up additional possibilities for promoting your book.

Likewise, consider the setting for your story. If you are writing about a real city or town, choose a place that is conducive to positive promotion and where the residents will welcome you and your book. If you pick a town that is too small and where there is little community pride, you won't be able to count on the residents for many book sales. If your story takes place in a major city that others frequently write about, your book might get lost in the shuffle.

The possibilities for building promotion into your nonfiction book are even more plentiful. Involve a lot of people while researching and writing your local history, for example, and list them in the book. Most of them will surely want a copy of the book. Profile early pioneers, and descendants will clamor to get one or more copies.

Maybe you planned to write a memoir featuring your experiences raising two autistic children. Through the process of developing a book proposal, however, you might decide that you could reach additional readers by also including a self-help or how-to element to your book. Offer guidelines for parenting children with autism, for example.

For a book featuring your life with cancer, add a section with tips for living with this disease. Maybe you've written a book of stories from your veterinary practice. You may attract more readers if you include a healthy pet guide.

Now, before you put the finishing touches on your book, go back and consider what you can add so that it will appeal to more readers. You might get additional readers for your children's story if you add a fantasy element. You may sell more copies of your dog book if you alter the focus from a fifty-page "me and my dog memoir" to a hefty book featuring thirty true dog stories. Consider adding a historic element to a love story, a hiking guide to a travel book, or a hands-on aspect to your children's home-schooling guide. Before completing your book, think about how you could change it to attract a larger audience.

I feel compelled to make the point again that just because you wrote it doesn't necessarily mean people will buy it.

Marcia Meier interviewed and quoted over twenty publishing/ literary experts for her book *Navigating the Rough Waters of Today's Publishing World: Critical Advice for Writers from Industry Insiders* (Quill Driver Books). She says, "I think that anytime you can include experts and their opinions with your own in a book, it's going to help drive sales. Many of those I quoted have helped promote the book in small ways—letting their own constituencies know about it, posting announcements in their blogs, sending me blurbs to put on my website, etc." And one of those who Meier featured interviewed her on a radio show.

While it is impossible to know how much of the book's success can be attributed to expert involvement, Meier's publisher is certainly using their names to promote the book.

When asked if she would recommend that authors involve others in their books, Meier said, "It can never hurt." But she warns, "It's a lot of work."

I can attest to that. Involving other people means tons of research, many disappointing moments, and a lot of follow-up work. It's an organizing nightmare. But for me, the end result is always worth the trouble.

Self-Edit Your Manuscript

Never publish or pay anyone to publish your book until it is absolutely ready. An important step to getting it ready is self-editing.

You want to make sure, for example, that your sentences make sense, that they are perfectly clear and say what you mean for them to say. Check your manuscript for clarity. Do you notice any inconsistencies or problems with the way it flows? You need to check for repeated words, misspelled words, misused words, redundancies, inconsistent spelling, and those dreaded passive sentences.

If you changed the name of a character or a place name in the process of writing this, be sure that you went back and made all of the corrections in all of the right places.

Do you know the difference between using *to, too,* and *two; than* and *then; whose* and *who's; your* and *you're; where, wear,* and *were; their, there,* and *they're; it's* and *its;* and so forth?

Find out the correct way to use apostrophes, semicolons, em dashes, etc., and be consistent in your manuscript.

Go back and make sure that your story or your instructions are reasonable and appropriate. I tell authors to write as if they are writing for someone from Mars. Don't assume that your readers will understand your intent—make your intent perfectly clear.

There's a whole lot to consider when self-editing, and it is definitely a step that must not be omitted.

Hire a Good Book Editor

Once you have done your best job of self-editing and proofing, hire a good editor and let her/him give your manuscript the once-over. If the editor runs into a lot of problems during her first go-through and if she has asked you to do quite a bit of rewriting, always turn it over to the editor again when you have finished your rewrites and final corrections.

As an editor, I've had clients write *over* me using the same bad habits that I attempted to help them correct. And then they publish the book and proudly credit me as being their editor. Now that's nice of them because I have done a lot for their project. But when they do extensive rewriting and introduce into their manuscripts new instances of muddy writing, run-on sentences, and additional errors and inconsistencies, it reflects badly on their editor—me.

Some authors skip the professional editing phase because they just don't want to spend the money. Some decide not to hire an editor because they don't want anyone else messing with their manuscripts—their voice. Some simply cannot see the necessity. Many authors hire the wrong editors—a retired college professor, their son's junior high English teacher, or someone at work who seems to have a way with words. Instead, professionals recommend hiring an experienced book editor.

The best editor for your project is someone who is also knowledgeable about the publishing industry. You can get so much more for your money if you work with someone who can advise you in preparing your manuscript for publication. It doesn't hurt if you can engage someone who knows something about your genre/topic as well.

An editor will charge anywhere from $500 to $5,000 (maybe more) depending on the length and complexity of your project and the condition of it when it goes to the editor. Start saving up now for this very necessary expense.

One author decided that my estimate to edit her 250-page book was too high, so she continued shopping around. It didn't take her long to find someone who would do the editing, sight unseen, for $75/hour, and he said that the job would take him five hours. The author was thrilled. She would be saving over $1,000, and the job would take much less time. She even contacted me to tell me that I really ought to change my editorial practices to be more in alignment with this editor as it was much more attractive to the author. I issued her a warning—strongly suggesting that she check this "editor" out before getting involved.

A few weeks later, the author contacted me and said that she had been scammed. The "editor" did nothing more than run an automatic spell-check over her manuscript and charge her $375. She was discouraged. She didn't want to pay for any additional editing. She decided to go ahead and have her book published without benefit of a professional editing. Consequently, she added to the abundance of poorly written books being published today by uninformed, unprofessional authors.

Get an editorial evaluation before hiring an editor. Some editors will look at a couple of chapters free and let you know the types of problems (if any) she sees there. She will also give you an estimate for editing your manuscript.

Warning: While there are databases featuring book shepherds and manuscript editors, I choose not to list them here because most of them are fee-based. In other words, the editor pays to be included. Sure, some of these editors are quite legitimate and very good. Choose from these lists, if you wish. But always get a sample edit before hiring any editor. A recommendation from an author you know and trust isn't a bad idea either.

Your pay-to-publish company might like your manuscript just the way it is—no editing necessary. But let me remind you that these companies are in the business of producing books, not necessarily well-written, editorially sound books.

You can choose to hire their editor. Some authors tell me that an editing job from a pay-to-publish company editor amounts to nothing more than a quick proofing of your manuscript—definitely not worth the money.

You've probably heard that traditional publishers have editorial staffs. Sure, if a publisher accepts your manuscript for publication, he will turn it over to his editorial staff in order to make it conform to their style. But if your manuscript is not professionally edited when you submit it for their consideration, they will, most likely, reject it.

Groom Your Book as a Marketing Tool

Don't make the mistake of allowing your book to be simply a book. Give it a job. Aside from the obvious responsibility of your book—to educate, inform, and/or entertain your readers—put it to work as a promotional tool. How? Include ordering and contact information inside the book. Some authors even have a few pages of order forms inside their books.

Have Your Publicity Photo Made

If you plan to do any promotion at all, you will need a publicity photo. You may want to commission a photo prior to completing your book so you can place it on the back cover. You'll also want to post it at your website, your blog site, and your social media sites. Don't forget to add it to your Author page at Amazon.com. (Read more about this in chapter sixteen.)

Once the book is published, you'll be asked for a publicity photo when you're interviewed for a newspaper or magazine article. You'll need it for posters when promoting your upcoming presentations. If your book is chosen as recommended reading, the web owner might want to use your photo. Some editors require a publicity photo to accompany the articles you submit.

I suggest going to a professional portrait photographer so you will end up with a crystal clear photo that will reproduce nicely for any occasion. Tell him/her what you'll be using the photo for. Typically, I would recommend shooting for professionalism in your photo. If, however, your book relates to baking, car repair, wine making, travel, etc., take at least some of the shots within the appropriate venue. You might pose in the kitchen wearing a chef's hat, in the garage working on a car, sipping a glass of wine, or standing in front of Westminster Cathedral. I use a professionally posed photo when promoting my line of writing/publishing books and a more casual photo (also taken by our photographer) with one of my cats for promoting my cat stories book.

As you select the photos that you want to represent you in a variety of venues, consider the persona you hope to portray before each specific audience.

Request Endorsements

If this is a second or third edition of your book, even if you are revising it, use comments from previous editions to promote this one. If you don't have a list of customer comments, book reviews, and professional endorsements, start contacting those who spoke favorably about this book in the past. Ask them to write a sentence or two reflecting their impressions of the book—what they liked about it, how it helped them, or made their life easier or more fun, for example.

If this is the first edition, give copies of the manuscript (or key chapters plus the table of contents) to key professionals in the topic or genre of your book as well as articulate friends and colleagues who could write meaningful and convincing testimonials. Post the best endorsements from the most influential professionals on the back cover. (Some authors even use endorsements from very famous people on the front covers of their books.) Also place a list of testimonials inside the book—generally within the front matter (somewhere between your table of contents and introduction or foreword).

Why would anyone bother to write an endorsement for you? For professionals in your field or genre, the motivation is *exposure*. If the subject of your book reflects this person's own expertise or interest, having his name published in your book affords him a good promotional opportunity. Friends and colleagues will do it in order to support your project or because they truly believe in it. Others may do it just for the thrill of seeing their names in print. So when you request an endorsement (or testimonial), do so with confidence because this is potentially a win-win situation for everyone involved.

Create a Website

Why do you need a website? It provides a place to showcase your book to thousands of potential customers/readers. A website is better than a calling card. It's more like a storefront window where hundreds of people can "walk by" at anytime of the day or night. If you want exposure beyond what you can get from your front porch, you need to build a website.

There are many website design programs available today. While some of them are certainly adequate, I encourage you to consider creating a site that's specific and unique to your project. Spend some time in research mode. Study other authors' websites. What do you like/dislike about them? Who designed the websites you prefer? Contact those designers and discuss possibilities. (Locate the name of the designer in the small print at the bottom of the home page.)

Determine the image you want to create with your website. What statement do you want to make? What message do you want to share? What do you hope to accomplish with your website? Once you've decided these things, go to work on the design.

Ideally, you would have your website up and running by the time you send out your prepublication promo. (See below.) In order to make this happen, you would likely need to start the process of building it before you send your manuscript off for the initial edit—in other words, before you finish writing the book.

If you only have time and/or funds to build the basic site, make sure that you include the following: a fabulous book page featuring the cover, a brief description, and ordering options. You'll also need an "About Us" page and a "Contact Us" page.

When time and funds permit, consider adding sample chapters, reader and expert testimonials, a media page (where you post book reviews and articles about you and/or the book), a blog, pertinent photographs (of you speaking, participating in a book festival, accepting an award, etc.), a schedule of your speaking engagements, a list of stores and websites where the book is available for sale, and perhaps a resource page reflecting the subject, theme, and/or genre of your book.

Some of you have your books showcased at your traditional publisher's or pay-to-publish company's websites. I still recommend that you develop your own website so that people can more easily locate you and your book without having to scroll through hundreds of others at the publisher's website in order to find yours. I know authors who have websites for each of their book topics/genres. For example, an author might have a website featuring their novels, one for their tax/finance books and other materials, and one for their how-to-edit books. It is a good idea to also create a website in your own name—*www.marysmith.com* or *www.johnnybrownbooks.net* . . .

When I produced the first edition of this book in 2000, I wrote that *almost* every author has his/her own website. Now I'd say that *every* author does (or certainly should). A website is a great way to introduce your book to people who are leisurely searching the web as well as those who are seriously looking for what you have to offer. Heaven forbid that someone learns of your book and cannot locate you at all via the Internet. Believe me, it happens. While planning your website, remember that the more you have to attract your particular audience, the larger the number of people who will find you.

Name Your Site Right

When you set up your website, you will be required to choose a domain name—a name that identifies your website. There's a right way and a wrong way to choose your domain name. I chose the wrong way when I set up my website. I decided to go with my publishing company name. Seems quite reasonable, doesn't it? But the name of my publishing company is not common. It is difficult to pronounce and impossible to spell. I shouldn't have even used it as a name for my publishing company, let alone a domain name. And I urge you to refrain from making this mistake.

In fact, I have righted my wrong this year by building a Patricia Fry website (*www.patriciafry.com*) to accompany my Matilija Press website (*www.matilijapress.com*).

When you choose your domain name for a site representing your book, consider a couple of things: the title, topic, and genre of your book; whether or not you plan additional books, if they will be in the same genre/topic; and whether you have achieved name recognition in your genre/topic.

If you plan to produce only mysteries, you might want to use the domain name, MysteryBooksBySarah, for example. Maybe you plan a series of books featuring outlaws. Consider naming your site, Outlaws.com or GunSlingerBooks.com. Perhaps your topic is herbs and you will only publish books and information on this subject. You could use the domain name, HerbsAndThings.com, HerbBooks.com or HerbsForYou.com, for example.

Some authors have multiple websites for various purposes—their local history books, their children's books, their editorial services, and their nonprofit organization. If you think you might want to do this in the future, see if you can secure several domain names you might possibly want to use in the future: AtlantaBooks.com, BeetleSkeetleChildrensBooks.com, IeditBooks.com, and BeetleSkeetleFoundation.org.

Most people, when they purchase domain names for future use, try to nail down all of those related to their current choice. Taking the BeetleSkeetle theme, you might secure BeetleSkeetle.com, BeetleSkeetle.org, BeetleSkeetle.net, TheBeetleSkeetle.com, and so forth.

Optimize Your Web Traffic

Search engine optimization (SEO) is the process of improving the volume and/or quality of traffic to your website. This can be done in a couple of different ways—you can pay to be listed first in searches related to your subject, or you can do it the natural way. A good webmaster can help you to develop the parameters within your website in order to naturally place your site high when certain keywords are used in a web search.

Ideally, your website will be among the top ten to come up in a web search by your potential readership. This will only happen if the searcher's keywords are prominent on your website and if these keywords are fairly unique to your book and your website. You and your webmaster must try to get into the heads of your readers and determine what keywords they are likely to use when searching for information on the topic or genre of your book. Make sure that each page of your site includes these keywords.

SEO experts recommend using key phrases as opposed to keywords, where applicable—"dog grooming," instead of simply "dog," for example. Be specific where appropriate. Use "Himalayan cats" or "feral cats" instead of just "cats."

I'm not going to recommend an SEO company that charges. If you want to check into paying for placement in Google and other major search engines, do your own search. Study the websites that come up. Always ask for references and check them out.

Of course, you'll also promote your website in every piece of promotional material you send out: on your business cards and brochures, in the articles you submit, in the comments you leave at various appropriate blog sites, in your e-mail "signature," and so forth. (Learn more about using a "signature" in chapter seven.)

To find out the most popular keywords Google has picked up from your website, use *www.google.com/sktool*.

Implement some of the free and fee-based keyword tracking sites to help you determine the best keywords to use in enticing your particular audience:

www.freekeywords.wordtracker.com
www.checkrankings.com

Solicit Prepublication Orders

During that lull between the time the camera-ready material goes to the printer (or your manuscript has gone to the publisher) and cases of your brand-new book arrive at your door, you should be taking orders.

To generate prepublication sales for the revised edition of my local history book, I created a brochure announcing the book and sent it to everyone on my mailing and e-mail list. I provided an order form and even offered a discount for orders received before the actual publication date.

I also made computer-generated business cards with information about the book and how to order it. I handed cards to everyone I met during those prepublication weeks. The orders resulting from these efforts helped me to pay down the printing bill by about $3,500 before my shipment of books arrived. (Note: I recommend not cashing customers' checks until the books are shipped or delivered.)

As Soon as Your Book Is Published

You'll discover that there's not much time to celebrate a new book because you'll be busy delivering and shipping books in order to fulfill your prepublication obligations. The first months, and especially the first days, after becoming a published author are busy, indeed. So the more organized you are—the more useful and logical strategies you apply to your project in those first weeks—the more potential you'll have for success.

Ship Prepublication Book Orders

Even before your shipment arrives, start typing labels and preparing padded envelopes and/or boxes for those prepublication orders. Log each sale in a ledger. When the books arrive, it's just a matter of slipping them into the packages, documenting the shipping date, and carting them off to the post office. Your next stop, the bank!

Run an Efficient Shipping Department

Like it or not, when you sign up to become an author, especially if you are also the publisher, you take on many responsibilities. Your writing room soon becomes a publishing office, a storage shed, and a shipping room. Even if you publish with a traditional publisher or a pay-to-publish service, you may still be required to ship books at least occasionally. Here are a few tips to help you adjust to this task.

Gather your supplies—I keep on hand bubble mailers (as opposed to fiber-filled mailers, which weigh more and thus cost more to ship), Priority Mail Flat Rate mailing envelopes and boxes for domestic and international use (free from the post office), a roll of clear packing tape, a roll of bubble wrap, and personalized business mailing labels.

While I know independent publishers who ship books only once a week, I ship practically every day. I advertise that books ordered from my website will be shipped within two working days. And I make sure that they are.

It may take a few trips to the post office to discover the best way to ship your particular book. For some of my books, first class is cheaper than book (or media) rate. If your customer is paying shipping, you want to send the books either first class or priority. For some of my heavier books, shipping in the Priority Mail Flat Rate envelope is less expensive and faster than first class.

I generally send review and complimentary copies via book or media rate, unless first class is cheaper. And this depends on the size/weight of the book.

When shipping several books in one shipment, pack them tightly—perhaps wrapped in bubble wrap—so they do not slide around on each other and get scuffed.

If you do a lot of shipping and/or you live a distance from a post office, you might consider leasing a postage meter to use in your home office (around $20 month). Or arrange with the U.S. post office to print postage from your computer. (I believe this excludes media rate packages.)

www.usps.com (U.S. Post Office website)

www.pbmeter.com (Pitney Bowes website)

Send Complimentary Copies to Key People

This is not just a nice thing to do; it is a smart move to make. Send complimentary copies to people who were key in the production of your book—your mentor, your book cover and design person(s), your editor, and your photographer, for example. Anyone who gave you significant material/information or quotes for your book should get a copy. Many of these people will purchase additional copies for friends and family. Consider sending copies to agencies that you noted in your resources page and/or that would probably have access to your customer base. I sent copies of my local history book to city hall and local museums, as well as the offices of the chamber of commerce, the board of realtors and the school district. I also donated a few copies to the library system. These donations resulted in hundreds of book sales over the years. The museums and the board of realtors sold copies of the book from their gift shops/offices. The county library system ordered over a dozen copies and paid full price. Practically everyone at city hall bought copies, and employees at all of these agencies/offices/systems promoted the book to visitors and patrons.

Put Copies into the Hands of Influential People

Nothing helps sales like having prominent spokespersons talking about your book. Do you have any idea how sales soared when Oprah introduced a book on her show? While your book may not get that kind of recognition, you can still increase your sales by involving the right people.

If your book is about parenting, send copies to well-known psychologists and family therapists along with a note suggesting they read it and recommend it to the families they work with. Ask each of them for a testimonial for your website (and future reprints), while you're at it.

Send a copy of your book featuring pet care for beginners to the directors of every major humane organization in the country (or at least in your region). They meet people every day who could use this book.

Send copies to anyone you know who writes for periodicals or hosts a radio or TV show. When I was writing magazine articles for a living, I often received complimentary copies of books from authors whom I'd interviewed. If I wrote on that topic again, I would generally mention the book. Subscribe online to HARO (Help a Reporter Out) at *www.helpareporter.com* and Reporter Connection at *www.reporterconnection.com/press*. You're bound to discover many additional journalists and experts who might be interested in reviewing your book or quoting it in upcoming articles.

The first edition of this book (*Over 75 Good Ideas for Promoting Your Book*) was popular with several publishers. They kept copies on hand to give to their authors. So I will likely send free copies of this edition to many publishers in hopes that they too will place orders.

Put your book into the hands of people who will recommend it to others—those with good networking skills. We all have friends who have a wide range of acquaintances and contacts and who love to talk up a good product.

Most of us give at least a handful of books away before we even start selling them—to those who helped us with the production of the book, for example. But it's also good practice to put copies into the hands of important people in your field and excellent networkers. Johnny Carson used to talk about Ojai on his late-night TV show, so I sent him a copy of my Ojai history book.

Canadian author Barbara (Bobbi) Florio Graham also took advantage of such an opportunity. She says, "Canada's prime minister is a cat lover, so I sent him a copy of *Mewsings/Musings* for his birthday." While he didn't acknowledge receipt of the book, Graham says about the practice of giving books away, "It increases awareness of the book and may lead to subsequent sales." She says, "I've had a couple of instances where people have told me they saw one of my books on the desk or table in the office of someone they were interviewing."

Expand Your Internet Reach

This is the perfect time to begin strategizing as to how you're going to attract visitors to your wonderful website. You've built a great showcase for your books. You've provided numerous resources and tons of information for your visitors. And you're using all of the right keywords. Now start and maintain a campaign to entice more and more people to your site. How?

- Add your website address to your brochures, business cards, e-mail signature (more about your "signature" in chapter seven), flyers, handouts, and all other communication and promotional material. Don't forget to include it on the back cover and the copyright page of the book itself.
- Post your URL in your blog regularly, when you comment at other blogs, and in your bio at the end of the articles/stories you submit for publication.
- Include your web address when you participate in forums and discussion groups.
- Make regular changes to your website. Search engines love to report something new. They go into immediate action when they become aware of additions and significant changes to your website. Do not delete material unless it is absolutely necessary. This type of change does not bode well with the search engines. But they are thrilled when you update or add new information, articles, resources, web pages, blog posts, and so forth.
- Get involved with some of the social media sites. Read more about this in chapter eight.

Use Your E-mail List Expertly and Responsibly

If your e-mail address book is like most, it contains the addresses of friends, family members, clients, customers, and many others. If you produce a newsletter or frequently send e-mails to specific groups of people (only clients, subscribers, friends who like animal e-mails, etc.) then you probably already have separate e-mail lists. I recommend that you create a list to use in promoting your book.

First, isolate all of those e-mail addresses for people who would likely be interested in your book. That could be just about everyone in your addressbook. But they might not all wish to receive your promotional material. E-mail each one asking them to respond if it is okay that you send them information occasionally about your book, news related to the subject of your book, and so forth. Create your list by adding only those who agree. Provide a sign-up option at your website. Offer a free e-book, report or subscription to your e-newsletter.

Now group all of the e-mail addresses you've been collecting at your site with those others who will be receiving your promo material. How?

Most e-mail programs have options for creating "mailing lists." Generally, you will find group mailing instructions and options under "contacts." Name your list. And whenever you want to send to this list, you can do so with a click of the mouse. When you send your e-newsletter, an announcement about an upcoming book event, news of an award won, etc., include an opt-out option in every e-mail. This means provide a clear and simple method for the recipient to unsubscribe. Unsolicited e-mail is spam.

Most professionals recommend that authors, who send group e-mails, do not use free e-mail programs that post a lot of advertisements in their outgoing messages. If this is how your e-mail program operates, consider establishing a relationship with another program for the purpose of sending out your newsletter and other promo material.

If you'd rather not handle your own mass e-mailings, you can hire a company to do it for you. They charge a wide variety of fees—generally, there is a setup fee and then you pay $15 to $25 month for a basic program. Here are a few companies that you can pay to do your mass e-mailings:

www.sandblaster.com
www.constantcontact.com
www.massmailingnews.com
www.amailsender.com

Promote Your Book Without Changing Your Lifestyle

You've heard and read often that the author is responsible for promoting his/her own book. You may wonder how this works, what it entails, how much time it involves, and whether you have the skill to actually sell copies of your book. Well, get ready for a dose of reality. You're about to come face-to-face with the scary monster you've been dreading—the actuality of book promotion.

No worries. I'm going to ease you into it gently. Now take my hand and don't be afraid. You can do this!

Create Amazing Promotional Material

You can't be everywhere at all times with your fabulous book. So you need something that can speak about your book when you're not present—something to send in the mail, to leave in stores, to hand to someone who is walking away, etc. Every book needs a printed sales pitch.

While you can use nice-looking business cards or flyers, my preference is a sturdy postcard with the book cover on one side and the book synopsis (one or two lines describing the story or focus of the book), description (ISBN, book style, binding type, number of pages/photos, price), and contact/ordering information on the other.

If you have room, include a few of your best testimonials. You may have to pare them down to one-sentence or even one-word phrases—

"Wonderful story," "Riveting!" "Highly recommended," etc. It is the name of the reviewer that is most important.

Since I am promoting several books as well as my editorial services, I've created a threefold brochure showcasing seven of my books as well as my editorial services. I also hand out business cards. But if I want to highlight one book, I will design a postcard.

Authors and publishers do a lot of promotion online, as well as off, so it is also necessary to create marketing material that you can send via e-mail. I like the personal touch. I'd much rather receive a personal note from someone who is sharing news of their recently published book than something that looks like an advertisement. In fact, if I open an e-mail and it looks like an ad, I usually delete it. On the other hand, if someone sends me an e-mail introducing their book, I will read it. I prefer that the e-mail includes an image of their book as well. Oftentimes, I will follow their instructions and click on a link to learn more about the book.

Be careful about offering a link only. Your potential customers are as busy as you are, and while they might read your personal note to learn a little about your new book, they may not take the time to click on a link.

Some authors promote their books through CDs. I'm still a little skeptical about whether people actually take the time to view promotional CDs and DVDs. Know your audience and whether they would be open to such technology. If your book focuses on trips you can take for great photo ops, your audience would probably appreciate a DVD showing examples. It seems like a lovely way to show off a book without killing trees.

I'm pretty sure that most brochures and other promotional material picked up at a book festival or other event are tossed before being read. If this is the case, it's even less likely that people will play a promotional CD or DVD.

We recommend *www.overnightprints.com* for business cards and promotional postcards. Also check with
www.printsmadeeasy.com
www.vistaprint.com

Use Testimonials and Endorsements in Promotion

A testimonial for an author is like a letter of recommendation to a job seeker. It's an endorsement for your book by someone other than you—perhaps, someone who has a following. These things do sell books.

Ask key people and influential friends to give you written testimonials that you can use in promoting your book. Authors and others who are marketing a business or themselves are generally eager to write a testimonial for other authors as it gives them additional exposure.

When reproducing the endorsement in your marketing material, list the name of the person and their expertise: Susan Markley, author of *Keys to Learning* or Benjamin Scolie, chef at the Regal Palace, for example.

Sometimes the testimonial isn't quite appropriate—it's too long or it includes personal comments from a friend. Most people, when they give you a written endorsement, will say, "Feel free to edit this to suit your needs." And, believe me, I do this quite often. If the person does not say this and you would like to tamper a bit with their comments because of limited space, for example, be sure to ask. You might even run the edited testimonial by the author for their final okay.

Keep adding testimonials to your book page at your website. Post them at your blog site. Use them in your promotional press releases, handouts, and brochures. And publish them in your newsletter. You might also post announcements reflecting significant endorsements in newsletters for some of the appropriate organizations you belong to.

(See chapter two for more about how to get testimonials or endorsements.)

Promote to Your Mailing List

Now is the time to use your mailing and e-mail list. Send your promotional material (postcard) to your mailing list. Send an announcement to your e-mail list. Include ordering information and a link to the book page at your website. (Note: I do not mean the home page of your website, but the actual book page where your book is prominently displayed.)

I know, I know, I just said that people don't always take the time to click on a link. They're more apt to do so if they know you, however, and if the link leads straight to your book page. I recommend providing, in your promotional e-mail, an image of your book cover, a succinct description of the book—its purpose and what it promises to deliver—as well as an organized list of specifications (page number, illustrations, price, binding, etc.)

Be sure to ask for the sale and make it easy and convenient for customers to purchase one or more copies of your book. If you're offering a discount to seniors, students, the military, or the first one hundred people who place an order, be perfectly clear in your communication. For example, don't say, "Offer ends June 29." Make sure potential customers know that you mean June 29, 2011. And always provide a way for potential customers to reach you with their questions either by e-mail or by phone or both. Neglect this simple step and you could miss out on unexpected opportunities—a bulk order (someone may want to know if you offer discounts on orders of one hundred or more) or an invitation to speak before your target audience, for example. Sure, it seems elementary, but I can tell you that I've known authors to omit contact information on their promotional material. And some of them do it purposely. They simply want customers to go to their website and place an order. They don't want to bother with a bunch of e-mails or phone calls.

Don't sabotage your success by going into hiding. Come out in the open, and I guarantee you'll be greeted in many interesting ways. If I had hidden away for fear of getting unwanted e-mails in 2006, I would not have received an invitation for an all-expenses-paid trip to Dubai, and I wouldn't have been the first woman ever to give a keynote speech at a Toastmaster's Convention in the Middle East. Nor would I have sold a dozen books (all I could carry with me) in less than an hour while there. (Read more about how to build an e-mail list in chapter two.)

Engage in Piggyback Marketing

Your mailing list is like gold to your business. Maintain it, add to it, and use it with respect. What if you could multiply your mailing list by two, three, or more? What if, instead of 324 names and e-mail and snail mail addresses, you suddenly had 600 or 1,000? It is possible, if you choose to "piggyback" with other authors/publishers. How?

Agree to send other authors' promo material in your book shipments and along with your mailings if they will do the same for you. But be discriminating.

Locate authors with books along the same lines as yours, but not in direct competition with yours. A few years ago, an author friend of mine was promoting a cookbook. I had a book on how to present a Hawaiian luau. We engaged in a fairly successful piggyback marketing program together.

Recently, a woman came out with a novel set in the Ojai Valley. She managed to weave her story through actual historic events. Her book is a perfect companion for my Ojai Valley history book.

Other successful piggyback partnerships might be a children's book and a parenting book, a book of poetry and one on how to write poetry, a memoir about a woman who adores cats and a book of cat stories, a book on how to give your home curb appeal and a gardening book, and even two novels in the same or similar genres.

Barbara Florio Graham is the author of three books, and she is a fan of piggyback marketing. She says, "Too often we consider others as competition rather than allies. I have a friend with a cat book who takes *Mewsings/Musings* to craft fairs and other events that I don't attend. I take her book to meetings where I display it along with mine." In her book, *Five Fast Steps to Low-Cost Publicity*, Graham suggests that authors combine forces with colleagues. A couple of ways to do that, according to Graham, is to do co-op mailings to libraries and arrange joint readings/signings at bookstores. She says, "The turnout at these signings can be small, but when more than one author is featured, more people come and book sales are higher."

Graham takes the concept of piggyback marketing to another level. She says, "I enclose a brochure and/or a promotional bookmark in business mailings even to my insurance broker, when paying routine bills and especially when renewing memberships." She adds, "Every book I sell contains promotional material for my other books."

Bundle Your Book

Bundling is different than piggyback marketing in that two (or more) books are actually "bundled" together as a package deal and offered at a bit of a discount. Again, choose books that are compatible and not competing.

If your book features wild animal stories from rural homeowners, you might want to bundle it with a book on bird watching or creating gardens that attract wild animals. If you have a book on home decorating in small spaces, you might couple it with one featuring home organizational tips. Maybe your book lists 101 low-maintenance flowering plants. See if you can find one on conserving water to bundle it with. Once you find such a book, contact the publisher and/ or author and ask if they will sell you a carton of books at a 20- or 30-percent discount. Bundle the two books for sale at your website and/or at book festivals, offering customers a discounted rate at which you are still making a little money.

Put Your Book in Catalogs

Mail order is big business, and depending on the type of book you have, catalogs could be a good way to promote it. Most of us get numerous catalogs through the mail every month. Some of them carry books—cookbooks, biographies, poetry books, story books, children's books, psychology/relationship books, spiritual/inspirational books as well as special interest books in the area of sewing/crafts, cooking, trains, collecting, and so forth.

You can create your own catalog of books at your website. You can enter your book into catalogs produced by your publishers'/ authors' organizations. Or find websites with catalogs related to your book's theme or genre and inquire about getting involved.

Recently, a catalog opportunity came to my attention from First Chapter Plus. For as little as $15, they will promote your book to nearly 35,000 librarians, booksellers, media, and others. Along with your ad (sized according to the fee you pay), they will also post your first chapter. Check them out here: *http://firstchapterplus.com/author.*

Don't overlook catalogs distributed by small companies. Someone who makes rag dolls at home and sells them through her own mail-order catalog might welcome the addition of a children's book featuring a rag doll character, for example. Find these catalogs through a Google search as well as in advertisements published in magazines related to the theme/genre of your book.

Here are a couple of resources to use in finding the appropriate catalog for your book:

Directory of Mail Order Catalogs
Grey House Publishing
POB 56
Amenia, NY 12501-0056
800-562-2139
www.greyhouse.com

The print book costs $395. It is available in the reference section at some public libraries. Or pay to use the online directory database.

National Directory of Catalogs
186 Fifth Ave.
New York, NY 10010
800-955-0231
www.oxbridge.com/NDCCluster/theNDC.asp
Additional catalog directory sites:
www.catalogs.com
www.catalogcentral.com

Talk about Your Book to Everyone You Meet

Anytime a conversation begins, there's an opening to talk about your book. I'm not suggesting that you bore everyone around you by talking nonstop about your book every chance you get. I'm trying to make the point that opportunities to tell people about your book abound, and you should take advantage when you can.

What do friends and acquaintances typically ask when they haven't seen you in a while? "What have you been doing?" They usually ask me, "What are you writing these days?" Don't let an opportunity like this go by—respond by mentioning your fabulous new book.

Likewise, when you're talking to a stranger on an airplane, while enjoying a latte at a coffee shop, while waiting in the veterinarian's office, or even while in line at the grocery store, bring up your book. A stranger might inquire about what you do. There's a perfect opening. Someone on your flight might ask if your trip to Buffalo was for business or pleasure—in which case you can say, "I was there speaking about my latest book . . . "

If there doesn't seem to be a good opening, create one. Ask the other person what he or she does or what their interests are. Watch for conversation directions that would segue nicely into the topic of your book. After someone says, "I'm happy to finally be doing something I love—something just for me," you might say, "I've just discovered the joy in that concept too, by publishing a book of my cat stories."

Don't monopolize the conversation. I hate when that happens. No, no no. Simply mention your book when the opportunity arises and the timing is appropriate. If someone seems interested, tell them more. If not, drop it. I find that someone who is uninterested might become interested after you express an interest in them for a while.

There are creative ways to bring attention to your book when you are out and about. Wear a tee shirt or carry a tote with a picture of your book on the front. Wear a button that says, "Ask me about my novel."

One author I know used to carry her promotional poster from out-of-state book signings on board her flight home. Inevitably, passengers inquired about her event, and she always sold a few books.

Carry Books Wherever You Go

Selling books is more of a hands-on activity than ever before. I often feel as though I hand-sell every single copy that goes out the door.

That's why it is important for authors to always, always have copies of their books with them at all times.

You never know when you're going to run into a former classmate or coworker, someone from church or from a group you once belonged to. Even your bank teller, postal clerk, business center owner, pet store worker, etc., might ask the key question to which you can respond by showing off your book. Carry your book in your purse, tote, or brief-case and pull it out and set it on the counter facing the clerk, waitress, receptionist, dental assistant, etc., each time you dig for your wallet or checkbook.

I've sold books out of the trunk of my car to patrons in my regular beauty shop, on the street to tourists who looked lost or who stopped me with a question, in line at the post office, in doctor's waiting rooms, on the Little League field, at my class reunion, and many other places.

Prepare a Thirty-Second Commercial (Elevator Speech)

Most authors love talking about their books. But not everyone loves hearing long commentaries even about a fascinating project. So how do you tell people about your latest and greatest book? Create a thir-ty-second commercial—a spiel to recite when you meet someone at a social event, in a business meeting, or on the street.

Include the topic of the book, the focus, and some of the benefits to readers. For this book, I might say, "It features over 250 low- and no-cost ideas for promoting your fiction or nonfiction book. As you may know, it is up to the author to promote his or her book, and this book is brimming with ideas for the bold as well as the bashful promoter."

For *Catscapades,* my book of true cat stories, I would probably gear my spiel toward the individual. If it is someone who doesn't have cats, I might pitch the book as "a great gift for your cat-loving friends." If she just adopted her first cat, I would talk about how heartwarming the cat stories are and outline a couple of the stories for her. If it is someone who has had a lot of cats in his or her life, I would probably give an overview of the book—stating that it features many cats that

I have adored over the years and that it will likely bring to mind some of those that she has known.

Tips: Never leave a conversation without exchanging business cards so you can add this person to your growing mailing/e-mail list.

Write and Respond to Letters to the Editor

Get publicity for your book by commenting on someone else's letter to the editor in a newspaper or magazine. Or write one of your own. You might notice a letter to the editor in a pet magazine on a particular topic that relates to your book. Maybe the writer has a cat that urinates on the floor outside the litter box, for example. You could respond to this letter (so that it is published in an upcoming issue of the magazine) by saying, "I resolved the problem of urinating outside the litter box by providing an empty litter box for my bad boy cat." Then either write, "I included this tip, along with many others, in my book *There Is No Such Thing as a Bad Cat* (Cat Kingdom Press)," or just add the title of your book under your name at the bottom of the letter.

Write your own letter to the editor based on items you see published in the newspaper or magazine. For example, maybe there's a controversy in your community about stone workers hauling rocks out of the river bottom to build stone walls. If your book is about protecting the habitat of animals, you might have something to say in a letter to the editor.

If you see a piece in a magazine about the increase in abandoned cats, write a letter to the editor with some resources from your book on feral cats. Be sure to mention your book as a reference for your expertise.

Promote Locally

There's a big world out there and we're even more aware of this since the advent of the Internet. But there's also a lot of potential for book promotion in your community. Rather than trying to reach out to the far corners of the world with news about your book, why not start on familiar ground—in your very own neighborhood.

Solicit Interviews in Local Newspapers

If you live in a small town, just the fact that "a longtime resident" or "local author" wrote a book could be news. And if your book relates to an aspect of your community, something trendy, something of interest to a wide audience, the editors may be interested in interviewing you for the newspaper.

It's more difficult to get press in larger newspapers, but certainly not impossible. Your story, "Hometown author pens book," isn't as newsworthy when you live in a large city. But you might be able to attract an editor's attention with a strong lead. Maybe you broke a record, broke out of prison, or wrote the biography of a famous celebrity. Editors of major newspapers might be interested in interviewing the author of books on these topics.

If your book is a novel, approach the book review editor at several large and small local newspapers. Or consider contacting the editors of newspaper columns that fit the theme of your book—seniors, pets, finance, travel, health/fitness, business, inspirational/religious, or the arts, for example.

At the very least, see if you can get your book mentioned in the calendar or entertainment section of the newspaper.

Don't wait to be invited to share the details of your new book. News of your book may not have traveled far enough to become reportable, yet. It's up to you to spread the word to and through local and county newspapers. Send an e-mail or snail mail press release or make a call to the appropriate editor and tell him or her about yourself and your book. Ask for what you want—a review of your book or an interview, perhaps. (Read much more about news releases in chapter six.)

Marian Clayton started the marketing campaign for her true crime, *Murder with a Twist*, by getting press in local newspapers. This was especially important because the story took place in her hometown in Colorado. She says, "I contacted reporters for newspapers in two different cities. They interviewed me and both wrote great articles that attracted a lot of attention. The publicity was great. I sold approximately twenty-five books in each community after the articles appeared. And," she says, "the stories created additional opportunities for promoting my book."

Clayton suggests to other new authors who want local publicity, "Find a reporter and speak directly to him or her. Tell the reporter about your book and ask for an interview. Always offer a copy of the book in case they want to read it before conducting the interview."

Arrange for Press in Regional Publications

There may be numerous large and small regional publications produced in your geographic area. Get lists from the local chamber of commerce and by doing a Google search. Also study *Writer's Market* (Writer's Digest Books). While some regional publications are for general audiences, others might specialize in sports, home and garden, fashion and beauty, children or writing, for example.

Study appropriate magazines to discover the type of material they use. Do they run book reviews? Do they publish human interest stories? Explore the possibilities and then contact the editors and ask for what publicity you want.

If you doubt the scope of regional publications, let me say that the listings for regional publications in *Writer's Market* span over fifty pages. That's around 175 listings, and these magazines reach anywhere from 20,000 to 450,000 readers each.

There are at least two dozen regional California horse-related publications, for example. There are at least twelve regional business publications for New York. Our county produces around fifteen regional publications on a variety of topics.

Get Involved in Local Events

Every community is a-bustle at one time or another with activities. There's the county fair, school events, book and art festivals, flea markets, cook-offs, community barbecues, auctions, wine-tasting events, and all types of fund-raisers. Many of these events provide opportunities for eager authors who want to sell books.

I once purchased a booth at the county fair with my local history book in mind. I designed my booth like an old-fashioned living room and spent the entire ten days talking to people about the early history. Of course, I also sold books—lots of them.

I've rented booths at numerous book festivals, flea markets, and art fairs. I gave historic tours via a trolley at our annual Ojai Day celebration for several years and sold books to many of the passengers.

Learn about upcoming local events in your town and around the county through the calendar section of local newspapers, your chamber of commerce, arts council, library, and so forth. If you are seeking events related to a specific theme, stay in touch with appropriate organizations and agencies. Get on related mailing lists, for example, for the music festival, camera club, historical society, quilting association, book clubs, etc.

Cherie Brant is the author of several Ventura County history books designed for longtime residents, newcomers to the area, history buffs, and tourists. Since her audience is local, she promotes locally through talks, events such as historic home tours, and book festivals. Along with her own promotional efforts, Brant has had a little help. She explains, "The first two books were printed by Del Sol Publications, and the owner helped with marketing to his business contacts and carried the book in his local store. Another one of my books was published in collaboration with the museum, and they helped to promote it. I also dealt for a while with a regional wholesaler who called on museums, gift shops, etc., in the county. And I went out and visited stores, museums, and other sites in the county that were not covered by the wholesaler."

According to Brant, "I sell a good number of books when I give talks on historic subjects to civic and social groups locally. I also donate historical tour packages to nonprofit organizations for their auctions and I give tours for the Museum of Ventura County."

She recommends to other authors who contemplate promoting books to a local audience, "Create a marketing plan that identifies every audience you can think of and the most effective ways to get your book in front of them. Look for places to sell your book that might not be traditional sites. Examples might be independent grocery stores and hospital gift shops."

Attend Local Group Meetings

Networking is vital to your book promotion success. That's why I urge authors to join and participate. You should definitely belong to groups related to the theme/genre of your book. But also consider joining more general groups for additional networking opportunities. I have sold books at my Toastmasters club meetings, chamber of commerce mixers, various writing group gatherings, businessmen's and-women's and retired businessmen's and-women's club meetings, Red Hat club luncheons, class reunion committee meetings, church auxiliary meetings, and others.

Just consider the benefits of participating in club and organization meetings. You're getting out of the house and away from the computer (always good for those of us who are addicted to writing). You're generally meeting new people at these gatherings. Each of those people knows many other people, and some of them just might be interested in your book on World War II, cats, celebrity pets, an inside look at automobile recalls, rumors about the *Dancing with the Stars* stars, or anger management made easy.

Offer Your Book as a Premium

If your book has an aspect that links it to a product or service, you might be able to sell thousands of copies at a discount to a related company. What will they do with these books? Possibly use them as premiums or in an employee-incentive program. Maybe your cookbook includes a lot of pork recipes. The owner of a local (or national) pig farm or pork packaging plant might be interested in using it to generate more customers.

Directors of insurance agencies, accountant firms, or loan companies might purchase your book on an aspect of local history in bulk to use in an upcoming promotional program.

How do you make this happen? Simply start approaching appropriate companies and agencies with ideas and prices. If you know that a local bank is observing its 100th anniversary in a few years, suggest that they use your book (on financial planning for the various stages in one's life or money awareness tips for college students) as a giveaway to new customers as part of their celebration. Maybe a world-famous resort in your city plans a major remodeling project. Offer them 500 copies of your historical novel at a 40-percent discount to hand out at their grand opening.

I've had companies contact me about purchasing copies of my local history book for attendees to conferences held in this community. In most of these instances, they paid full price.

Give Home Parties

Although it may seem bizarre to consider inviting people over to hear a spiel about your book in Tupperware-party style, it certainly is a way to get exposure. Call friends and acquaintances in all parts of your county and ask them to invite friends and neighbors in for a book party.

Make it an evening of fun; give a demonstration related to your book, bring costumes, and ask guests to help you act out parts of your story. Serve refreshments and offer door prizes. If your novel is set in the South around the Kentucky Derby, for example, serve mint juleps in glasses with racehorses painted on them. Present glasses to those who purchase books or the person most beneficial to your group performance.

For an event featuring a humorous memoir, do a reading or tell some of the stories from the book. Serve an appetizer reminiscent of your attempt, as an eight-year-old, to make Froot Loops brownies. And give each attendee a genuine *bug-a-boodle* just like your childhood invention.

A talk about your book on ghost busting and local hauntings would certainly attract a lot of people to a home party. Bring some eerie music and black lights for atmosphere and be sure to devise a surprise for those guests with strong hearts.

Tip: Invite other local authors to bring their books so guests will have more titles to choose from.

Sell Books at Yard Sales

I often put a table of my books out for sale when I have a yard sale or when a neighbor or friend is having one. Since yard-salers are specifically looking for bargains, it's difficult to get full price even for brand-new, hot-off-the-presses books. I take this opportunity to unload some of my damaged books—those that were slightly squashed in the mail and returned, those sitting on bookstore shelves for a long time, and those that got a little dusty while stored improperly in the garage.

Make a sign indicating that the books have been discounted by 25 to 50 percent and that the author's autograph is free.

Tip: Keep books in the shade. The hot sun will warp them and you'll have to discount them even more.

Go Door-to-Door

People still walk through neighborhoods selling their wares. If you have a good personality and if this mode of commerce appeals to you, load your wagon with books and start pounding the pavement in search of sales. If nothing else, this experience may give you material for your next book.

I have spoken with authors who have been quite successful selling books door-to-door. They say that it is such a unique concept for most residents that neighbors buy books for the novelty of it.

Submit News Releases and Tip Sheets

Every new author hopes to get press for his or her book. We all want newspaper publicity. But how do you go about getting it? People, upon seeing an article about me and one of my books, often ask, "How did the reporter find out about you?" Those who don't know about promotion and publicity are surprised when I say, "I contacted them and asked for an interview."

Yes, that's how it works. The author approaches the newspaper reporter, editor, or columnist. And the tool most frequently used in these instances is a news release.

Contact Newspaper Editors through News Releases

To sit back and wait for the public to find you and your book is to never be found. You, as the author and/or publisher, must reach out. You have to draw attention to yourself in order to be noticed. How? One way is through newspaper publicity.

As we mentioned in chapter five, you should send news releases to daily and weekly newspapers initially to introduce your book. But also submit them periodically to get additional publicity. Announce upcoming book signings, speaking engagements, awards, your volunteer projects related to the theme of your book, and so forth.

Locating newspapers today is much easier than it was when I started getting involved with book promotion. I spent hours in local libraries scouring phone books and various directories in search of contact information for newspapers throughout the United States. Today, authors use some of the great online newspaper directories (listed below) to get listings for the geographic areas of their choice. Some of the directories even include newspapers worldwide.

Get the name of the appropriate editor or columnist and devise a news release to send. (See sample news release in the appendix.)

As I said earlier, the fact that there is a new book on the market isn't exactly news by today's standards—at least not outside of the author's hometown. If you submit a news release simply announcing your book, it may be ignored. It's time to get creative. Give editors something new, different, unique, and definitely of value to their readers.

For a nonfiction book, consider the problem/solution news release. Identify a common or current problem or concern that your book addresses. If this problem touches a large segment of society, it is probably worth confronting publicly. Succinctly represent a solution or remedy to this problem in your news release and it will probably get the attention of several editors.

For example, maybe your book features how to photograph children and pets. You might send a press release around Easter or Christmas with this heading, "Do Your Family Photos Lack Personality?" or write, "Tips for Capturing Your Pet's Personality in Home Photos."

If your book focuses on resources for seniors, you might write, "Is your elderly loved one getting all of the help available?"

Introduce yourself as the author of *Finding the Personality in Your Photos* and a professional photographer or as a social worker/senior advocate and the author of *Little Known Resources for Seniors*.

What does a news release get you? Sometimes the editor will run it as is. She might be inspired to contact you for more information or an interview and a photo shoot. When this happens, I urge you to contact bookstore managers in that geographic area, letting them know that your book will be featured in their local newspaper. Suggest that they order books to have on hand in case there is a buying frenzy. If you can get it together in time, you should be able to mention the bookstore in the interview, which would make the bookseller happy, indeed.

I make it sound fairly easy to get press. The truth is that, in this time of stiff competition for print space, your news release may flat be ignored. Many are. So make sure, when you strategize, that you address the needs, interests, concerns, and passions of the readers for that particular publication or column.

It is more difficult to get press related to a book of fiction, but not impossible. Read chapter fourteen to learn how to make news. This is an excellent promotional technique for authors of fiction or nonfiction books.

Here are a few ideas for getting a newspaper editor's attention with a press release for a novel or a children's book. Timing is everything. Send press releases to announce a book signing or upcoming presentation. Submit press releases when news is slow. Obviously, it's hard to predict the news as breaking news can occur at any time. Consider the news—is there anything going on that's related to the theme of your novel or children's book? Tie your press release in with current events and seasonal holidays. (Read more about promoting by season in chapter twenty.)

As you can see, sending news releases should not be a helter-skelter type of activity. As an author, you must pay attention to the news, fill a need, and practice impeccable timing.

Newspaper directories:

www.newspapers.com
www.onlinenewspapers.com
www.thepaperboy.com
www.50states.com/news

Not only is Carol White an expert when it comes to teaching authors how to write successful press releases, she uses them to promote her own book, *Live Your Road Trip Dream*. She says, "I have developed my own list of media people who work in my genre, but I sometimes also use press release services." She explains the nature of a press release. "It's an offer of information to a specific set of media people who would be interested in your news story for their particular set of readers." While most authors think of press releases in terms of newspapers, White points out, "You could also direct your press release to people involved in magazines, radio/TV, websites, blogs, or those who might book you to speak at their companies."

When issuing a press release to a newspaper editor, White suggests, "Go for quotes around a breaking news story or a lifestyle-type article depending on your area of expertise and the topic of your book." There's also the announcement-type news release. White says, "I always use targeted press releases when we're going to appear in a locale." And she suggests to authors, "Don't overlook specific holidays that relate to your book." She shares this: "Just prior to Memorial Day, I released a story through PRWeb (a press release service) about how to keep gas prices down while traveling and had over 45,000 views/looks and 563 actual journalist or consumer readings."

Use News Releases to Reach Niche Magazine and Newsletter Editors

There are thousands of magazines and newsletters reflecting a variety of subjects. Some of them relate to the theme of your fiction or nonfiction book. Use news releases to get publicity for your book in appropriate niche periodicals.

A news release for a magazine might look different than one for a newspaper. Magazine editors are looking for articles and filler material. They might have columns to fill. A news release to a magazine should be targeted. In other words, study the publication so you know what type of material they use and how it is presented. Then decide how you can break in. You might suggest that the editor interview you and run a book review. (Read more about book reviews in chapter nine.) Maybe they will include information about your book in their Announcements, News Bytes, or What's New section. Or you might even suggest that you write an article for the publication. (See more about writing articles for magazines as a way to promote your book in chapter fifteen.)

I find newsletter editors more open to receiving news releases than newspaper editors. While the circulation for newsletters is often smaller, newsletters are generally more narrowly targeted. So all one hundred subscribers to a newsletter focusing on doggie dress-up would, presumably be interested in your book featuring the latest in fashions for dogs. Nearly every subscriber to a newsletter addressing diabetic cooks will be potential customers for your book on easy meal makeovers for diabetics. Do yourself a huge favor and do not disregard the newsletter market when it comes to promoting your book.

Magazine Listing Directories:

Writer's Market (Writer's Digest Books)

www.writersmarket.com

www.woodenhorsepub.com

Newsletter Directories:

www.newsletteraccess.com

www.ezinehub.com

www.ezinelocater.com

Send News Releases to Columnists

If your book is conducive to a specific column type found in newspapers, magazines, and newsletters, by all means use press releases to contact the columnists. Always address a columnist by name. Follow their guidelines for writers or for submitting news (generally located at their website). Be specific with the information in your news release and your presentation suggestions. Very often, if your material is appropriate and timely, they will publish it as is. Sometimes, however, they will take it in a whole different direction—slant it a whole new way. And that's okay. It's press, after all.

Here are some ideas for getting publicity through columns. Choose appropriate columns in magazines, newsletters, and newspapers that are read by your projected audience. If your book features the best fishing spots in the western states, seek out regional, fishing, sports, outdoor, men's, nature, boating, camping, and RV publications, for example. Look for columns in other publications reflecting outdoor activities in the west: outdoor sports, nature, or those that are specific to fishing. You might find these in regional, travel, ecology, and general publications.

Maybe your book focuses on rainy day, summer day, and snow day activities for kids. You'll probably seek out magazines and newsletters for parents. Also consider columns in regional, religious, educational, children's, and even general publications, which address parents, grandparents, daycare providers, and teachers.

For a novel, choose periodicals and columns that tackle some of the issues in your story. These might include publications related to health, pets, religion, spirituality/inspiration, family, men's, women's, relationship, psychology, New Age, hunting, crafts . . . Use your imagination and your research skills to the max.

I've promoted my writing/publishing books to public speakers who want to turn speeches into books, seniors who might consider writing their memoirs, retirees who want to earn extra money writing, people interested in writing their spiritual experiences, young writers, businessmen and women who want to publish books on their expertise, and of course, those who are passionate about writing and are seeking direction.

Promotion for my luau book appeared in magazines and newsletters read by folks interested in Hawaiiana, cooking, barbecuing, the pork industry, and entertaining.

(Use the resources at the end of the listing above to locate appropriate columnists.)

Try an Online Press Release Service

Some professionals say that sending press releases is an obsolete practice—that you will get more action by posting your press releases online. And there are sites designed just for that purpose. Some of these press release sites used to post and distribute your news releases for free. Now, many of them charge, at least for some of their services.

Use online press release sites to learn how to write a good news release. Check them to get ideas for your own press release topics. And consider posting and/or distributing your press releases through a company only after comparing services, prices, and reach. Find out what others are saying about these press release services.

Some authors post their news releases at their own sites and in their blogs. I haven't seen it personally, but I understand that there are editors and journalists who go out in search of new books to review and authors to interview on certain topics. So it doesn't hurt to be prepared by posting a press release.

See sample press releases in the appendix.

Here are a few press release sites to consider:

www.prweb.com
www.prleap.com
www.prfree.com
www.free-press-release.com
www.prbuzz.com

Many authors use press releases services or PR sites. Some of them are free, and others have some pricey packages. Cliff Ball is promoting three novels using a wide variety of methods, including two press release services. He says, "I've been using these services for about two years and probably issue a press release every other month." While some services have different policies, Ball says, "I provide the press release, and the service submits it all over the Internet and to distributors." Does anyone receive and read these randomly distributed press releases? According to Ball, "I occasionally get queries from book reviewers or requests for interviews." He knows that people are noticing his press release. He says, "I can check the hits at the PR companies' websites—there's a display of where they're from."

Ball uses these services because, as he says, "They know what they're doing, and I believe they have a greater reach than I do." He adds, "My goal is to get people to buy my novels."

Create Tip Sheets

A tip sheet is a list of four to eight tips, facts, or ideas that are designed to teach, inform, or entertain. Magazine and newspaper editors use them to fill space. Some editors pay for these "fillers."

You could create a tip sheet related to just about any nonfiction book topic. For a book on selling your house, you might consider devising a brief list of simple tips explaining how to create curb appeal when selling a house, a list of facts about real estate in a particular region, or a list of ideas for choosing the right realtor, for example.

For a book on travel, you might develop a tip sheet for traveling with your pet, a list of family-friendly hotels, or tips for more efficient packing practices.

If you've been writing articles and blogging about the theme of your book, you may already have material that you can use in several tip sheets. Just remember to keep them short—in the 100- to 300-word range. Always include your name, title of your book, and contact information.

Submit them much the same as you would a news release or an article—addressing the correct editor at an appropriate publication.

What do you get out of writing and submitting these tip sheets? Publicity for your book and added credibility in your field. (See sample tip sheet in the appendix.)

Use Your Website to Sell Books

We've already established the importance of a website for authors in this publishing and bookselling climate. Like it or not, we have entered the digital age; we are deeply enmeshed in the era of technology. Publishing a book without bothering to build a website is like throwing a party without inviting guests.

How can a website enhance your book sales? How can you enhance your website to encourage more sales? Let me count the ways.

Showcase Your Book

The purpose of your website is presumably to showcase your book and/or to call attention to your expertise. When working with your web designer, make sure that you present a clear message to the audience you hope to attract.

Let's say that you are a jelly and jam expert who has recently published a book called *Marmalade and Other Delicious Preserves.* You want to make sure that your website visitors know immediately that this book exists, what it covers, and that it is for sale. You also want to present yourself as an authority on making preserves, jams, and marmalades. How would you accomplish this?

Make sure that the book cover speaks—no, *shouts*—"I am a jam and marmalade cookbook." Place the book front and center. If there isn't a photo of you on the book cover wearing an apron and happily stirring a pot on the stove, place one somewhere on the home page.

If your name is well known in the industry, display it in large letters (probably your name on the book cover will suffice). You might also state somewhere near your photo (if it isn't already printed on the book), "As seen on the KRS TV *Cooking With Jane* show."

Do you see how we have done more than just sprinkle the page with advertising facts? We have created a "case" for the value and credibility of this book. Anyone visiting this site now knows what he or she initially needs to know about your book and you.

Anyone interested in this book or knowing more about the author will click on "About Us" or "About the Book" and, perhaps, even the "Buy This Book Now!" button.

Post Testimonial at Your Website

Most likely, you'll continue to receive comments and feedback from customers and reviewers. If not, be sure to ask for them from time to time. Don't discard even a word of these comments. In fact, get permission to use and edit them (if necessary) and post them at your website for the whole world to see.

I post client and student comments as well as customer comments at my website and provide convenient links from each page to the testimonials page.

Design a Fantastic Book Trailer

A book trailer is a video advertisement for your book. If you're creative and technologically adept, write your own script and shoot your own trailer. If not, hire someone such as the folks at Circle of Seven Productions: *www.cosproductions.com*. They charge anywhere from $300 to $10,000 for a video featuring your book. Plan to spend at least $500 for a decent book trailer.

The features you'll want to embrace when designing your book video or trailer are similar to those you would consider when writing a book: Make sure that it relates to your book and that it will hold the interest of your audience. Your book video should capture the viewer's attention within the first few seconds. It should be intriguing, informational, and/or entertaining. But in order to be effective, it must also be brief—one to three minutes.

You could film yourself or someone else reading from your book; show still photos or video related to the book while narrating and recording background music. Or you could actually have someone act out scene clips from your book.

By now you should know your audience—what do they want/need from your book. These are the points you want to feature in your book video ever so briefly and with extreme appeal.

For more about book trailers, including a tutorial and some examples, check out *www.squidoo.com/booktrailers* and *www.darcypattison.com/marketing/book-trailers*.

Once you've produced a book video, where do you show it? You can always put it on YouTube and your own website. Play it on your laptop while you are signing books at local bookstores and promoting your book at book festivals. Enclose a DVD of the book trailer with the press kits you send and hand out. One author of a true crime book created a book trailer for the homepage of her website. When you open her website, the trailer starts. It is quite impressive.

Additional book trailer designers:

www.movingstories.tv

www.authorbytes.com

Award-winning author Marilyn Meredith uses book trailers to promote her Deputy Tempe Crabtree mysteries (Mundania Press) and her Rocky Bluff P.D. crime novels, which she writes under F. M. Meredith, (Oak Tree Press).

She says, "I think that a book trailer can give a reader a feel for the book that they might not get any other way. It also definitely piques viewers' curiosity about the book." While she still promotes her books through many other avenues, she says, "Book trailers are one more way to let people know about your book. I think it's all a part of the whole—I do a lot of online promoting, and I do see a jump on Amazon buying since I had my trailers designed.

Several times, I have had readers tell me that they bought my book because of the trailer."

Where does one post book trailers? Meredith advises, "It's important to display your book trailer in as many places as possible. When I go on a blog tour, I make sure my trailer is available on each of the blog sites. My trailers are all on my website and YouTube. Of course, when I have a new one, I always let everyone know via Facebook, Twitter, etc."

She suggests to other authors, "Be sure the trailer looks professional. And remember, they'll only help if you promote them in many places." To see Meredith's trailers, visit *http://fictionforyou. com.*

Create a Podcast or Webcast

Record your message or read passages from your book as a podcast (audio blog) and post it at your website for others to download onto their iPods or MP3 player or listen from their own computers. Subscribe to an RSS feed so that whenever you post a podcast at your site, your audience will be alerted. (Learn more about RSS feed and various servers in chapter fifteen.)

You can record your audio message or presentation through an external microphone connected through one of the jacks available on the back of your computer. Or you can use a service outside of your computer. In this instance, you can call from anywhere and record your podcast. Here's the link to such a server: *www.bookmkr.audio-acrobat.com.* As with a blog, you can podcast daily or weekly. You might want to set up a page on your site just for podcasts.

While some authors charge for their informational podcasts—those containing seminar material, for example—others use podcasts as free publicity for their books.

A webcast is an audio or video broadcast over the Internet. Many radio and TV stations use this method to reach people via their computers. The webcast differs from the podcast in that it is broadcast to those who subscribe and is not downloadable. The data is sent in real time. However, there is an on-demand process used by some webcasters, meaning that people can listen to or view the broadcast at their convenience. The webcast is used a lot in the business world to conduct meetings among telecommuters, for example.

Podcasting is a better option for authors attempting to promote their books as it is more convenient and less expensive to set up, send, and receive.

For more information about podcasting and webcasting visit these sites:

www.how-to-podcast-tutorial.com
www.wisegeek.com/what-is-a-webcast.htm
Additional Podcast Hosting sites
www.podbean.com
http://libsyn.com

Turn Your Website into a Valuable Resource

Many authors neglect to make full use of their websites. They simply post their books and provide a little "about the author" information. I suggest using your website to lure people who need additional information and to keep them there. How?

If yours is a nonfiction book, post articles and resources related to the topic of your book and then do a lot of promotion to get people to come to your site. Think about it, don't you spend more time at sites where you can find answers to your questions, resources you can use, and relevant articles? Don't you give the owners of these sites more credit than those who simply showcase a book on the subject? Aren't you more apt to purchase books from someone who you feel has more credibility in the field?

If your book is fiction or a children's book, consider offering links and information related to your genre or set up a forum where people who like to read mysteries, suspense, horror, etc., can converge and talk about the genre.

Be sure to establish an active blog. And an entertaining book trailer and/or regular informative podcasts can and will keep visitors at your site a little longer too. (Read about how to establish a blog in chapter fifteen.)

Forum software to get you started:

http://zoho.com/forums-software

www.ninjapost.com

http://thinkofit.com/webconf/forumsoft.htm

Google and Yahoo can set you up with a discussion group:

http://groups.google.com

http://groups.yahoo.com

Get Your Site Listed in Online Directories

When I want to research websites related to a specific topic/genre/theme, I often do a "directories" search. In other words, I seek out appropriate online directories because they typically provide links to numerous sites within that category.

Often, my search involves directories of sites for writers and authors. When I find a good directory, I ask to be included. I suggest that you do the same. Get your site listed in all of the major directories in your topic or genre. When people are seeking information or material on the topic of your book (best fishing spots, how to raise a show dog, teaching children Spanish, business management, etc.), your site will be among their list of options.

Set Up a Merchant Account

I dragged my feet for a long time before finally getting a merchant account system. And I am awfully glad that I finally caved. I can now take credit cards through my website as well as for books sold at book festivals and for client work. I've had my merchant account now for about nine years, and I've never had to pay the monthly fee out of pocket. Sure, the fee comes out of my profits, but I am selling books that I may not have sold without the merchant account.

Check with your local banker about their merchant account fees. Most likely, you'll want to choose a merchant account company that specializes in website accounts such as USA Merchant Account at *www.usa-merchantaccount.com* or Total Merchant Services, *www.merchant-account-4u.com* or Intuit Business Center *www.intuit.com*. Ask other authors which merchant account companies they use. Do a Google search to locate others. Check their contracts and policies carefully.

Use an E-mail Signature

You've seen those mini ads at the bottom of e-mails from friends, colleagues, and professionals. They're called "e-mail signatures," and people use them to promote their credentials and advertise their books and/or services. Most e-mail programs offer customers the option to create their own signatures. Once you've established your signature, it can be set to accompany every e-mail you send. If you'd rather it not appear in personal e-mails, simply delete it before sending the message.

Locate the signature option in your e-mail program. It's under "Options" at Yahoo. Type in the information you want to use. This generally includes your website address (es), title of your book(s), and any relevant affiliations.

Consider your signature a business card that is included with each of your outgoing e-mails.

I can tell you from firsthand experience that people do respond to the information in your e-mail signature. Several times, I have had colleagues or authors respond to my e-mails with comments or questions about the information in my e-mail signature. They might say, "I am impressed by your credentials—do you speak to writers' groups?" YES! Or "You've published thirty-one books? Do you work with other authors? Could I hire you to help me with my book?" YES! Or "Patricia, I visited your articles page at your website and I'd love to publish your article on small talk. Would you accept $500 for one-time rights?" YES!

If I want to know more about someone who has sent me an e-mail message, I always look for a *signature* that includes their website address, their company name, their book title, etc.

Sign Up for Affiliate Marketing Programs

Some people believe that affiliate marketing programs bring more visitors to participating websites. What is affiliate marketing? It's a process through which one website is groomed to drive traffic to another. It's a marketing strategy whereby businesses are rewarded for bringing customers to other sites. It's similar to revenue sharing or working on commission. You pay your affiliates a commission to send traffic to your site. While some agreements are based on the number of people who visit the site, others require that the visitor purchase something before the affiliate is paid.

Amazon.com created one of the early Internet affiliate programs. It works like this: You allow Amazon to post a link at your website. For every customer who clicks on that link and subsequently orders your book from Amazon, you get an additional percentage of the transaction. SPAWN is an Amazon affiliate, and we receive small checks from time to time.

There are basically three types of affiliate programs: Pay-per-sale (as the merchant, you pay affiliates when a sale is made), pay-per-click (you pay affiliates based on the number of visitors who click on the link), and pay-per-lead (you pay when a visitor takes some specific action—signs up for something, for example). Some merchants sign up many affiliates in order to generate many more visitors and sales.

While affiliate programs are fairly simple to set up, there can be a lot of work involved in locating appropriate and compatible affiliates, negotiating an agreement that works for everyone, and monitoring the number of clicks, sales, etc., generated from each affiliate. If it gets to be too much, you can hire an affiliate network to keep track of everything. These networks can also help you to set up your affiliate program. Some charge an annual fee for their services. The initial cost could be $1,000 or more. A less expensive way to go is to purchase traffic-tracking software for around $300.

The point of getting involved in an affiliate program is to attract potential customers to your site. So you'll want to become affiliated with the right individuals or groups. Use the directories below to locate appropriate affiliates.

Affiliate program directories:
www.affiliatescout.com/
www.100best-affiliate-programs.com
www.linkshare.com

Promote Your Book through Social Media

Social media describes the growing number of sites which were originally designed to help people connect with former classmates or military buddies, for example. Classmates.com came into being in 1995, and the social media site concept evolved from there. MySpace was launched in 2003, Facebook and Twitter in 2006. Now the various social media sites accommodate friends and family members who meet up for fun and stay in touch as well as businessmen and women who want to network with their colleagues, customers/clients.

Aside from the well-known sites, there are numerous targeted sites for hobbyists, collectors, aficionados, and experts in various fields/interests. Check them out here. Chances are, you will find a social media site focusing on the theme or genre of your book. There are social media sites for a variety of interests. Find them listed at *www.stumbleupon.com* and *http://en.wikipedia.org/wiki/List_of_social_networking_websites.*

Are social media sites a good idea for authors? I've always advised authors to become known to their audiences—to get out and speak to them, hand-sell books to them, do signings, participate in book festivals, etc. Social media is another great way for authors to mingle with their readers and to connect with them at a more personal level.

Join Facebook, Twitter, LinkedIn, Etc.
Many countless authors—both new and experienced—use various social media sites for additional exposure. Each of these social sites

offers a slightly different twist and method of getting the attention you desire.

Facebook is a social networking website that helps you stay connected to friends, colleagues, and even customers: *www.facebook.com*. What are some of the secrets to using Facebook so it works for you? Participate and become active. It doesn't have to take a lot of time. In fact, those authors who experience success on Facebook, typically spend just fifteen or twenty minutes every day or every few days interacting through Facebook. As with most things worth doing, it is quality rather than quantity. You could respond immediately to every message that comes from your Facebook account or you could collect the messages and respond and post once per day. Respond to the messages you receive, of course. But also reach out and comment on other people's Facebook pages. Use your Facebook page to note your upcoming events, awards/recognition, milestones, accomplishments, big sales, etc. But be careful when it comes to promotion.

While blatant promotion is frowned upon at most social media sites, there are many ways to exploit your book using personal, personable, and interesting tactics and techniques. In order to use Facebook and other social media sites as a sales tool, you must approach it as you would your daily blog or an article or speech on the subject of your book. Rather than harboring grand expectations of selling large quantities of your book simply by mentioning it at your Facebook page, strive to inform, educate, and/or entertain your social media "friends" and "fans." Be helpful. Give. Share.

It is important that you adopt a mind-set of altruism. If you establish a social media account and then expect to sell thousands, hundreds, or even dozens of books, you will not be a happy camper. If, on the other hand, you embrace social media as another great way of getting exposure—becoming known in your field/genre—you, most likely, will experience some measure of satisfaction and even success.

One thing I like about Facebook (and some other social media sites) is the fact that you can post photographs. There's nothing like candid, fun, personal photos to engage others.

I mentioned earlier that there are social media sites in many categories. You can join a site related to reading and books, history, investing, art, travel, needlework, politics, fitness, and many other topics. But you can also join or start interest groups through Facebook. Learn more about joining and starting Facebook groups here: *www. facebook.com/apps/application.php?id=2361831622&b*

Once you sign up for Facebook, you can pay to advertise right there on your page. Fees vary, depending upon whether you want to pay a flat fee (say $25/day) or pay per click. Devise your own ad and choose your fee base here: *www.facebook.com/advertising.* Learn more about Facebook and how to use it to your benefit here: *www. facebook.com/get_started.php*

Most experts recommend becoming involved with more than one social media site. Here are a few to consider. Twitter is a networking site for microblogging. When you have a Twitter account, you can type 140 characters at your page whenever you want—daily, multiple times each day, weekly . . . Your posts are then sent to all of your "followers"—those who have signed up to receive your messages.

While there is a lot of, seemingly, frivolous tweeting going on at this site, some authors find Twitter most useful for making brief announcements, teaching, sharing, directing people to their blogs/websites/recent book reviews, etc. Sign up here: *http://twitter.com.* For more information about using Twitter, go to this site: *http://twitter-howto.com.*

Use Twitter's search function to locate people who are interested in your topic: *www.search.twitter.com.* If you want to know more about how Twitter can help you promote your book, check out this site: *http://business.twitter.com/twitter101*

Linkedin is billed as a professional networking site: *www.linkedin. com.* This site combines some of the best features from both Facebook and Twitter. And then it has added some designed specifically to assist the businessman or woman. I like this site for authors because there is less chitchat and more opportunity for focused conversations and more meaningful business relationships. Learn more about LinkedIn here: *http://learn.linkedin.com*

If you want to network with other authors, here are some social media sites for you:

www.jacketflap.com
www.redroom.com
www.authornation.com

The latest thing in social media is *www.google.com/buzz*. It is designed to integrate photos and videos as part of the conversation for more intimate and interesting networking.

Not only is Penny Sansevieri a publicist and a marketing expert (*www.amarketingexpert.com*), she practices what she teaches to promote her own array of books. And using social media is a big part of her promotional toolbox as well as those of her clients. According to Sansevieri, "One social media site is no better than the other, but you do want to keep current. Don't engage in social media abandonment." She says, "Get on as many social media sites as you can, including your own blog, and then use them—whatever you have, keep them updated."

She also advises that you have the right message. In other words, "Think about what your audience wants or needs and give it to them."

Sansevieri understands that some authors just don't want to clutter up their lives with a lot of social media obligations. She suggests, "If you only have Facebook, Twitter, your own website, and a blog, that might be enough. Experiment a little. Those that will pay off for you are the ones that you should use."

Participate in Forums and Bulletin Boards

Many organizations have forums wherein, as a member, you can post questions and comments, discuss problems, make announcements, share resources and so forth with like-minded people. There are also forums and boards related to your topic/genre open to the public—no membership required, although you must register for most of them. Most have rules involving no rude or lewd behavior or comments, no blatant advertising/promotion, and so forth.

Here is a directory of forums and boards: *http://directory.big-boards.com/*

To locate boards and forums in your topic/genre, do an Internet search using keywords, "forum" + "cats" or "bulletin board" + "gardening," for example.

Join Online Discussion Groups

There are discussion groups on practically every subject imaginable. Participate in those that seem to attract your particular audience. But beware; the hosts of most of these groups and message board sites discourage self-promotion. And many of the groups are for members only.

The best way to use these groups is to offer benefit of your expertise whenever appropriate. Here are a few ground rules:

- Comment on the posts of others.
- Make suggestions where appropriate.
- Be kind and generous.
- Offer news and resources.
- Avoid negative or belittling comments.

Visit often in order to learn more about what's going on in your field and what your audience wants/needs. You may, in fact, discover resources, perspective, and even some quotable remarks to use in future books and articles on your topic.

Most discussion groups and boards need hosts. Search around and you might find opportunities to host an appropriate discussion group, message board, or chat room. This might be fun, and it would certainly add to your credibility in your topic/genre.

Here's a large directory of online discussion groups and message boards:

http://wallphone.com

Solicit Book Reviews

How often has a book review sold you on reading a particular book? I think we have all been swayed by enthusiastic reviewers. And we're eager to get our own amazing books reviewed. But few new authors realize the vast opportunities for getting book reviews. This chapter provides information, resources, and encouragement for getting your book reviewed over and over again.

Get Your Book Reviewed Many Times Over

One excellent way to ensure that your book is noticed and becomes known is through book reviews in key publications. Some major reviewers do not want to see the finished book. They will only review a book before it is published. In this case, two to four months prior to the publication date, you send them a bound manuscript or camera-ready computer printout with cover. These reviewers review books primarily for the library market.

Many books today do not qualify for prepublication reviews as these reviewers do not generally review self-published or pay-to-publish books or books that are not suited to the library market. (Read more about what makes a book suitable for the library market below as well as in chapters two and twenty-three.)

Once your fabulous, attractive, perfectly edited book is published, you can get it reviewed many, many times. All you have to do is ask. It's up to you to seek out review opportunities among appropriate consumer and, perhaps, trade (or genre) publications. This includes magazines and newsletters as well as newspapers and websites.

Many publications have book review sections or columns. There are book review websites. But beware, some of them charge. There is no reason to pay for a book review. I don't typically recommend having your book reviewed at book review sites because they post so many reviews that your book can get lost among them. An exception would be a niche book review site—your book is a romance novel or a young adult fantasy and you have found a review site specific to this genre. Your novel or even your book on building doghouses or the latest cancer cure would probably go unnoticed at a site where they review dozens of books each week on all subjects and genres.

Locate magazine listings in *Writer's Market*, WritersMarket.com, and WoodenHorsePub.com. Use *Literary Market Place* (*www.literary-marketplace.com*), *Ulrich's International Periodicals Directory* (*www.ulrichsweb.com*), and *International Directory of Little Magazines and Small Presses* (*www.dustbooks.com*) to find additional publications in your genre/topic. Order a mailing list of magazines and newsletters. (Learn more about ordering and using mailing lists in chapter two.) Seek out newsletters and obscure magazines on your topic through an Internet search. A diligent search may reveal directories of publications in your genre/topic. And don't neglect to scour large magazine racks in mega bookstores or magazine stores to locate appropriate publications.

I also recommend studying the websites of other authors who write in your genre or on your topic and see if they post their reviews. Contact some of the same reviewers and tell them about your book.

Tip: turn your book into an e-book and offer it to reviewers instead of sending out so many copies of your print book. Some reviewers prefer receiving paperless versions of the books they review. And what a savings to you!

There are a variety of types of book reviews and an equal number of methods of soliciting them. Rosie Sorenson is the author of *They Had Me at Meow: Tails of Love From the Homeless Cats of Buster Hollow*. She solicits book reviews in every appropriate magazine, newsletter, or website she hears about. In fact, she figures she has given away over a hundred review copies so far. And those reviews are selling books. According to Sorenson, "One review resulted in over sixty books sold. From another review, I sold twenty." She suggests using experts to help you get reviews. "Get some good blurbs from people who are prominent in your field and use them in your e-mail pitch to reviewers."

Christy Pinheiro solicits tax instructors to coordinate reviews for her study guides. She explains, "They find students who are about to take the tax exam and they are offered a free study guide if they just agree to leave a review on Amazon or barnesandnoble. com." According to Pinheiro, "The reviews really help sales, even those that are not 100 percent positive. Glowing reviews always sound fake." She explains, "I got a four-star review from one candidate who said, 'This book is really great, but the font is small and difficult to read.' That review has been marked as the 'most helpful,' and it boosted sales from day one. Customers like to hear pros and cons, and apparently the small font was a drawback that they could handle."

Steps to Getting Book Reviews

Locate appropriate publications. Some magazines have book review columns. Others might run reviews only occasionally. If your book is a guide to bed-and-breakfast inns throughout the southern states, for example, address the travel editor of a magazine or newspaper. A book on how to make gourmet designer coffee drinks would probably appeal more to the foods editor than the general editor or book review editor.

Once you have a few publications in mind, contact the appropriate editors with information about your book and a brief bio. But first, check each magazine's website for book review submission guidelines. If your book qualifies (not all editors will review self-published or pay-to-publish books), send the items they request in the way they require—e-mail or snail mail.

If you don't hear from the reviewer within a month or two of having sent the preliminary information about your book, follow-up with an e-mail or phone call.

If your book is requested, send it along with a sample review or two, if you have some good ones. Some reviewers like to use material from previous reviews or your back cover copy when writing a review. Sad, but true.

Once an editor requests your book, follow up until the review is published. You might think the reviewer doesn't want to be bothered, but I can tell you that, more than once, my phone call to a reviewer resulted in a prompt (and, by the way, favorable) review.

Before sending out a review copy, mark the book "review copy." Reviewers will sometimes sell review copies on the Internet or take them to bookstores for credit. It has happened to me and several of my colleagues. If the book doesn't sell in the bookstore, it may be sent back to you for a refund. Now there's a lose-lose situation for the author.

I stamp "review copy" on the flush edges of the pages before sending books out to reviewers.

Save copies of the published review to send to other reviewers and to use in other forms of book promotion. Post reviews at your website. Use sections from them in devising promotional handout material. Use portions of reviews on your testimonials pages or on the cover of your future revised edition. And be sure to ask all reviewers to post their reviews on your book page at Amazon.com.

Your Book as Recommended Reading

You've probably already found several websites on the topic or in the genre of your book. Isolate those that have "Recommended Reading" pages. If it looks as though your book will fit in with the others there, contact the web owner and ask if they would consider your book for inclusion on this page. My writing/publishing-related books are recommended all over the Internet on numerous writing and publishing-related websites. Likewise, my book of cat stories is listed as recommended reading at several cat sites.

Some sites even have bookstores set up from which they actually sell other people's books and e-books. Think about it, the more your book is recommended, the more exposure it's getting. And exposure leads to sales.

Solicit Author Reviews for Amazon

You may notice, when you visit Amazon.com, that there are reader reviews on many of the book pages. Presumably, you will have your book at Amazon.com. Sometimes readers or even colleagues will post reviews at your Amazon book site in order to get exposure for their own books. (You can also comment on other authors' Amazon pages for books that relate to your topic/genre.) Some of the reviews are legitimate comments from actual readers. But mostly, they are comments and reviews that book reviewers have posted after they have written and posted a review at their site or in their publication.

Be sure to ask book reviewers to post their reviews of your book at Amazon. Those stars you get from reviewers are pretty significant.

But keep an eye on the stars that appear. I once had a reviewer say in her review that she gave my book five stars. However, she mechanically gave me one star. I know exactly how this happened. If you're in a hurry when you are clicking on the number of stars, and if you click too soon, some of the stars will fall off. I have tried and was never able to contact this reviewer to ask her to repair the damage. And no one can do it but the original author.

(Learn more about getting your book on Amazon.com in chapters sixteen and seventeen.)

Discover Value in Book Review Sites

I generally warn authors against soliciting reviews at book review sites because of the volume of books being reviewed. It is difficult, if not impossible, to have your book showcased effectively at these sites. There's just too much competition. On the other hand, you can never get too much exposure for your book. While I don't believe that a review on a major book review site will generate many (or any) customers, it does provide exposure. The more times a reader sees your title or hears about it, the more apt he or she is to purchase it. Some professionals believe that publishers scour book review sites in search of the next best seller. Some say that multiple reviews at the various review sites impress librarians, and they'll be inclined to order your book.

So go ahead and solicit book reviews at some of the online book review sites. It might be worth your while in the long run.

Online book review directories:

http://acqweb.org/bookrev.html

http://dir.yahoo.com/arts/humanities/literature/reviews/

www.stepbystepselfpublishing.net/free-book-reviews.html

Arrange for Book Signings

I think that every author dreams of having many successful book signings. We imagine signings where we are mobbed by our readers and end the day with writer's cramp. The fact is, this scenario is generally true only for celebrity authors the caliber of J. K. Rowling. As a virtually unknown author, you may have just a handful of friends show up at your signing and sell a dozen books. And that's only if you have worked hard to promote the event.

Set Up a Book Signing

Book signings aren't always at bookstores. I've known authors to sign books at libraries, pet stores, pharmacies, department stores, kitchen stores, nurseries/garden centers, and flower shops. Why couldn't you do a signing for a book on vintage motorcycles at a bike shop, for a book on wine making at a winery, or for a children's book in a toy store? Be creative in your search for book signing venues.

Do you really know what makes a book signing successful? A multitude of sales isn't the only criterion, especially for a first book by a new author.

I've seen authors leave book signings bordering on depression because they didn't sell the number of books they expected to. What many first-time authors don't realize is that they may have gained something almost as valuable as sales—exposure.

In order to get that exposure, however, you have to put in the promotional effort. As Debbie Puente, author of *Crème Brulée and*

Other Custard Desserts, says, "The worst book promotion mistake you can make is to do a signing that is not advertised."

When you schedule a book signing, find out if publicity is up to you or if the store manager will take care of it. If they're going to do it, ask how the signing will be publicized. Ideally, they will send news releases to all area newspapers, publish an announcement in their customer newsletter, post a large sign advertising your book and the date of the signing, and display your books in the center aisle during the week of the signing.

If they don't do these things, do them yourself. And also consider booking yourself on a radio or TV show local to the area before the event and/or speaking before a large group of your readers. Also deliver promo material about the book to the store and ask them to include one with each purchase during the month of your signing.

You can (and should) augment these promotional efforts. How? Invite everyone you know to the signing. Yes, send out personal invitations. Some of your friends and associates have already purchased your book. Invite them anyway. They may want to buy another copy as a gift. Some friends will come just to support you. And that's good, because people draw people. Bookstore browsers are more apt to join in with a crowd than to approach someone who is sitting alone at a table.

Send invitations to groups, businesses, and organizations related to the topic of your book. If your book features home office decorating tips, send invitations to small business organizations, local companies (large and small), writers groups, and office supply stores. For a book on gentle care for the elderly, send notices to hospitals, senior facilities, churches, and hospice organizations. Ask them to post the notice on their bulletin boards and include it in their newsletters.

It's always a good idea to plan a book signing well in advance so organization leaders have time to get the information in their monthly newsletters. Send a follow-up reminder the week of the event to your list of friends and acquaintances.

Use bribery. Announce in your invitations and flyers that there will be magic acts, a celebrity guest, a demonstration, gifts for everyone, games and prizes, or something else designed to attract people.

Diana Zimmerman is the author of *Kandide and the Secret of the Mists*, a young adult fantasy. She has sold thousands of copies of her book through over 300 bookstore signings in dozens of cities. It is typical for this author to have a line for three hours when she's signing books, which is highly unusual for someone who is not a big name author. What's her secret?

She comes to each town with a definite plan, which anyone can implement. Since Zimmerman's audience is children, she visits local schools during the day, and the students visit her that evening at the local Barnes and Noble. She says, "I call this plan the Golden Triangle: Schools, Kids, Booksellers."

She compares her bookselling success at book signings with that of others: "I can't tell you how many times I have been to multiple-author signings and the other authors just sit there. I was in Oregon for a signing, and a really well-known author sold only fourteen books. I sold forty—all that the store ordered." What makes the difference? Zimmerman goes out and creates a buzz about her book before the event, and her audience duly responds.

She admits that, "Barnes and Noble loves me because I create long lines of kids and sell books. Well over half the people who come in for *Kandide* buy one or more other books."

(Read more about how this author gets gigs at schools in chapter fourteen.)

Book Signing Tips for Authors

- Don't wait for an invitation. Take the initiative and approach local bookstore owners and managers of businesses related to your book topic. Offer to give a presentation along with the signing.
- Attend other signings for two reasons—to support fellow authors and to find out what works and what doesn't.

Over a month prior to the event:

- Send notices to organization and club leaders related to the theme/genre of your book letting them know about your signing and/or presentation. If they send monthly newsletters or have monthly meetings, this will give them plenty of time to inform their members.

- Either order or make sure the bookseller orders copies of your book from the publisher.
- Arrange for radio/TV and/or speaking engagements in the city of the book signing.

3 ½ weeks before the event:

- Double check on your book shipment. Speak to the shipping department manager to make sure the books will ship on time. (I can't tell you how many publishers, printers, and fulfillment companies have ruined the perfectly good plans for a book signing by falling down on the job and not getting books shipped on time.)

2 ½ weeks before the event:

- Send press releases with a photograph of yourself and your book cover to all newspapers within a forty-mile radius. Tell about your book, yourself, and what your presentation will consist of. Include your phone number. An editor may want to contact you for more information. (Do this even if the bookstore manager said he will do it.)
- Arrange for a radio interview to coincide with your signing.

10 days in advance of the event:

- If the staff doesn't plan to do so, make posters and flyers or bookmarks advertising your signing and deliver them to the store. Ask clerks to include a flyer or bookmark with each purchase.
- Offer to design a store display of your books.
- Send e-mail or snail mail invitations to the local addresses on your mailing list—friends, neighbors, coworkers, relatives, acquaintances, etc. Remember to tell them about the special gifts, entertainment, or other surprise you plan.

One week before the event:

- Know ahead of time what to expect. Will you have a microphone? Lectern? Table at which to sit for signing? Will you have to arrange for these things yourself?
- Check the store stock. If you are the publisher, find out how many additional books you will need to bring.

A few days before the event:

- Send e-mail reminders or make phone calls to those locals on your mailing list.
- Show up for your radio/TV or speaking engagement.

The day of the event:

- Dress to stand out in a crowd, but not so dramatically as to distract from your presentation.
- Be prompt. Arriving a little early will give you time to settle in.
- Bring handouts such as related articles, a report, or a sample chapter. When I sign *Quest for Truth*, I offer free copies of my article on meditation walking. For *The Mainland Luau*, I give away a recipe I devised that makes oven-roasted pork taste like kalua (pit-roasted) pork. I had magnets made to give away with my book of cat stories.
- If you have promised gifts, bring enough for a group of thirty to fifty.
- Reach out to people; don't wait for them to come to you. Hand copies of your book to folks in the audience or who visit your signing table. If things are slow, walk around the store and hand books to customers. It's easier to engage them in conversation when they are holding a copy of your book in their hands.
- Keep track of the number of books you autograph in case there is a discrepancy.

After the event:

- Send a note of thanks to the store manager and staff.

- Attend other signings and note what works and what doesn't.
- Realize that signings and presentations will rarely exceed your expectations and hardly ever meet your highest goals. But anytime you are given the opportunity for this sort of free publicity, you are making headway in your promotional efforts.

Have a Combined Signing

Because two (or more) people will draw a larger crowd than one, some authors pair up for signings. Choose your partner(s) carefully. It should be someone whose book complements your own because you want to attract people who are interested in your topic/genre. If his book is on car racing and yours features how to write a thank-you note, neither of you will benefit much from the presence of the other.

Avoid paring with someone whose book is in direct competition with yours. Few people would buy two books on parenting a two-year-old or parallel books about building birdhouses. Complementary books might include one about attracting butterflies to your yard and one featuring yard care tips for the handicapped. A duo with a book of animal-related poems and a novel about a dog might entice the same buyers. You could promote your book on writing thank-you notes along with one featuring how to make paper products, and the car racing book might sell to the same audience as would a book featuring biographies of sports figures.

Give Demonstrations

Attract more interest for your book signing by doing something unusual—a demonstration, for example.

When Debbie Puente first came out with her book on custard desserts, she combined her book signings with demonstrations showing how to make crème brûlée. She always drew a crowd for these presentations and sold a number of books too.

When Teddy Colbert demonstrates how to make a succulent wreath, she always sells copies of her book, *The Living Wreath*. I saw demonstrations by both of these authors, and I bought both of their books.

Not every book is as conducive to demonstrations as these two. What can you do to jazz up a presentation for a novel? Come to the event with scripts and a few props—hats, feather boas, a smoking pipe, a fancy cane, a fake moustache, and so forth—and involve members of the audience in acting out a scene in your book. Can't you just imagine how much fun you (and your audience) could have with this?

For a business book, have volunteers take on roles depicting some of the lessons in the book—how to handle an irate customer, for example, or how to work through a managerial problem.

Always send a thank you to your host for a book signing. And offer additional publicity for both the store and your book by blogging, tweeting, and posting at your Facebook page after the event. (Read more about using social media networks in chapter eight.)

Debbie Puente is a cookbook author. When Renaissance Books published her book, *Elegantly Easy Crème Brulee and Other Custard Desserts*, she went right to work promoting it by demonstrating how to make crème brûlée. She says, "Tasting samples helps sell. Look at Costco! Handing out samples gets conversations started, and once someone stops to talk to you, there's a good chance that they will buy your book." She says, "I always sold more books at demonstrations."

When I asked where she conducted demonstrations, she responded by saying, "Mostly upscale cooking stores like Williams-Sonoma and Sur La Table. But also lots of independent bookstores and cooking schools, expos, fair . . . I even went to the Fancy Food Show in New Orleans. If I was invited, I would go."

"Preparing for a demonstration took some planning, especially when I was traveling," she says. "If I had a kitchen at my disposal, I would make my samples the night before and leave them in the refrigerator. But after many TV appearances and as the book's popularity grew, people began doing this for me."

Demonstrations certainly create extra work for the author. But Puente advises others who have books conducive to demonstrations, "Anything worth doing is worth doing right, so get into the mind-set that you will have to work hard to sell books."

Get Out and Talk about Your Book

I still maintain that one of the most effective ways to sell copies of your book is to personally introduce it to live audiences. If it is a novel or children's book, you can do readings, puppet shows, or solicit audience participation in acting out the story. But do not attempt this without either a natural talent for reading/presenting or having taken appropriate classes. I know one author of a young adult fantasy book who hires an actress to do readings from her book during presentations. And I've heard many others who should.

If yours is a nonfiction how-to, informational, or self-help book, consider presenting workshops on the topic. This might include, family budgeting, self-publishing, dog grooming, caring for an elderly loved one, weight loss, a particular craft or something motivational, for example.

The most successful presentations—those that sell the most books—are those where the author teaches, leads, guides, motivates, or somehow touches/moves audience members rather than simply talking about the book.

Become a Public Speaker

You can't sell a book that no one knows about. One way to spread the word is to go out and talk about it. If you aren't entirely comfortable with the idea of speaking before a group, you might want to take steps to overcome your fears or your distaste for public speaking.

When I published the first edition of *The Ojai Valley: An Illustrated History*, I called everyone I knew who belonged to a local club or organization and offered to speak before their groups. I contacted the chamber of commerce and requested a list of local clubs and organizations. I called their organizers and set up speaking engagements. I also got in touch with the directors of local schools, libraries, and museums.

Those who attended my presentations told others about them and word of mouth brought me many other speaking opportunities, such as through Elderhostel, special local events, and conventions held in our city.

"Sure," you might say, "it's easy to talk about local history. But what do you say about a novel?"

You have a lot of creative options. You can tell how you came to write and publish it. A writer's life is still a fascinating topic for most. Dress up in costume reflecting a character in your story—the period, the style—and then relate part of the story and read some of your more intriguing passages. But do not attempt to read from your book unless you are quite accomplished. Not many people can engage an audience while reading out loud. Practice reading out loud, record yourself reading, and continue practicing until your performance is riveting and flawless. Some authors hone their speaking and reading skills, especially where their children's books are concerned, by joining storytelling groups.

I believe I've seen practically every example of poor performances by authors giving readings. Maybe if you attend workshops, book signings, and other events where authors will be reading from their books and speaking, you will learn what to and what not to do. You'll be exposed to excellent readers as well as those who mumble, stumble over words, read too fast, speak in monotone, and commit many other infractions that make it impossible to get anything out of their presentations.

When I first came out with the local history book, I enjoyed going out and talking about it; and the audiences seemed to respond to my talks. After a while, however, I felt a need for improvement. In an effort to further hone my speaking skills, I joined a Toastmasters club.

And I strongly suggest that you do so: *www.toastmasters.org*. I participated heavily in my club—eventually earning my Advanced Toastmaster Silver. And I continually practiced speaking within and outside of the club.

Now I travel all over speaking to authors at writers' conferences and at writers' group meetings throughout the United States. I've addressed thousands of people on behalf of my various books. In 2006, I was invited to Dubai, all expenses paid, where I was the first woman ever to give the keynote speech at a Toastmasters annual convention in the Middle East.

Accepting public speaking engagements often means free press for your book. The club or organization will usually submit news releases announcing the meeting or event. Sometimes there's a follow-up article recapping the presentation. Be sure to send your photo and bio to the publicity chairperson. But be prepared to take over the promotion of the event in case the club representative hasn't developed a promotional strategy.

How many different opportunities are there for promoting your book through speaking? If you have a book of poetry, participate in poetry slams. Read your children's book at schools, libraries, and bookstores. For your nonfiction book or novel, consider speaking before businessmen/women's clubs; civic organizations; special library events; corporate, organization, or theme-related conferences; workshops through local spas or other businesses.

Most of these activities come with back-of-the-room sales opportunities. In other words, you can set up a table and sell books to those in attendance.

I advise that you stand tough and squelch any fears or distaste you might have for public speaking because this is a fabulous way to sell books. People are much more apt to buy a book from the author once they develop a rapport with him or her and know a little inside information about what the book offers and how it came about. I can tell you this firsthand.

Many times, I've seen people thumb through my book, simply look at it in passing, or pass it by altogether. After hearing me speak on the subject of my book, however, those same people will often eagerly purchase it.

Here are sites listing conferences in a variety of topics/genres:

http://shawguides.com

www.allconferences.com

www.bvents.com

Karon Korp is the author of *Remembering Our Spiritual Journey Home: The 12 Keys for Awakening the Memory of Who You Are and Why You Are Here* (Magic Mountain Press). Her main promotional activity is public speaking. She says, "Since my book came out in 2002, we've been to roughly one hundred events in forty-two cities to promote the book at conventions, expos, trade shows, workshops, and book signings."

Korp focuses much of her energies and efforts on live presentations because, as she says, "It became clear early on that if we were to focus solely on book sales, we would starve. So we expanded our offerings to additional personal development and New Age products. This brought more clients to our company/presentations/booth/website." She says, "When speaking publicly it is nice to sell books, but my motivation is to touch people's lives and offer them a perspective that enlightens and assists their own process of self-discovery."

How does Korp discover these speaking opportunities? She says, "I research events in my genre, look for established opportunities with centers that have a market—a following. I also utilize key contacts in cities where I've built an audience."

Her advice to others is, "Network and don't leave the promotion to someone else."

How to Get Speaking Gigs

Start with your own clubs and organizations. Ask friends and colleagues about their affiliations. Study the front pages in your local telephone book for a list of local clubs and organizations. Check with the chamber of commerce. Look for club and organization listings in your local newspaper. And, of course, use our dear friend Google to locate groups in your area that use speakers.

Eventually, branch out and arrange to speak outside your area—in neighboring counties or while traveling, for example.

Find out who the program chairperson is and contact him or her with a pitch letter—something similar to a press release. (See a sample of a pitch letter in the appendix.) Include information about yourself, a little about your book and some specific ideas for your presentation. Be sure to provide your publicity photo. (See chapter two for more about your publicity photo.)

Consider the audience when devising your list of possible presentations. If I'm speaking to a group of authors who have one or more published books, I will give a completely different talk than if my audience consists mostly of beginning writers who only dream of someday publishing. I design a very different program related to local history when I'm talking to schoolchildren than I do when addressing members of a Rotary Club, for example. And my history presentation for tourists is different than it is for members of the local historical society or for docents at the museum.

Get Paid to Speak

Once you hone your speaking skills and begin to enjoy giving presentations, create a program that people will pay to hear. Sell your book as a manual or guide for the course. I know a gentleman who is preparing a book on volunteering and plans to earn a living making presentations to large companies using his book as the text.

Charge a fee for conducting workshops related to the topic of your book—writing, baking, entertaining, resume-writing, disaster preparedness, photography, and so forth.

If you're interested in being a paid speaker, sign with a speakers' bureau in your area to help you land engagements. Or get involved with a national speakers' bureau. There are many, many choices in national and international speakers' bureaus. Here are just a few: American Program Bureau, *www.speakersbureau.com/sonly.htm;* Fine

Speakers Bureau, *www.finespeakers.com/speaker-inquire.html*. You may want to start out on a smaller scale with a regional speakers' bureau designed to locate local engagements for you. Some writers groups sponsor speakers' bureaus.

To find a speakers' bureau near you, do a Google search using keywords "speakers' bureau" + your city or state name.

Sing for Your Supper

Get passage on a cruise line or room and board at an exotic convention spot by offering your presentation or workshop to their guests for free. I've known a couple of authors who have worked this type of deal. If your book covers an interesting, enlightening, entertaining, or even rather provocative topic, you might be able to land a contract.

What are some of the subjects that might help you get booked at a resort or on a cruise ship? I can imagine many possibilities within the realm of foods (shipboard diet tips for those with food issues—diabetes, allergies, etc.), art (body painting for lovers), fitness (couples' exercises), psychology/therapy (meditation walking techniques for greater relaxation and rejuvenation), photography (how to take more amazing travel photos), and more.

Dress Up Your Talk

Sure, you can stand at the lectern or even wander around the stage and simply speak to your audience. You can involve audience members in a variety of ways. And you can also bring in props to enhance your presentation. I encourage props, handouts, change-of-pace activities, and even video recordings and PowerPoint presentations as part of your program.

I once watched an elderly woman use handheld signs with prompts printed on them. It seemed a bit primitive, but she pulled it off as quite charming, actually.

I've watched speakers carry various items on stage and use these items to make points during the presentation. When the items are foreign to the topic of the talk, they can pose quite a curiosity for audience members who see these things waiting in the wings to be used.

I have forced myself to learn how to use a PowerPoint projector and I've had fun using my own diagrams, photographs, and bullet points during presentations. This is an excellent way to make a point, and it helps you to stay on track with your message.

Some years ago, I purchased a PowerPoint projector, and I've traveled with it numerous times, very carefully protecting the sensitive (and expensive) bulb from damage. Today, however, you can purchase palm-size digital PowerPoint projectors. And many venues have projectors for your use—all you have to do is ask.

Sell Your Books on the Road

You can help pay for your trips by selling books while traveling. Whenever you pull into a town, stop at local bookstores and/or appropriate specialty shops, introduce yourself, and offer to autograph your books. If the store doesn't already carry your book, show it to the manager and ask if you can set up an account with them.

Plan ahead and arrange for signings. Be sure to see about doing interviews on local radio/TV while there as well.

If you're traveling by RV, show books to fellow campers. Ask if the operators of camp stores want to purchase a few copies to place for sale.

Read your book on the plane or train—have extra copies in a carry-on to sell to passengers.

When you stop to eat, set your book on the table and see if you can engage others in a conversation about it.

When my Ojai history book came out, I toured many cities throughout Southern and Central California and placed copies in several museum gift shops and independent bookstores between Solvang and San Diego. You really can sell more books through personality than through mail or e-mail.

Give Seminars and Workshops Across the United States

If your book encompasses a topic that can be taught, consider developing a seminar or workshop. Maybe you've written about an aspect of retirement, customer relations, or how to be more organized. Imagine yourself traveling around, teaching people the principles of your book.

Many books are conducive to workshops and seminars. The business world has conferences that need speakers. But there are conferences that reflect a variety of other topics as well—pets, relationships, gardening, home remodeling or maintenance, fashion, art, foods/cooking, autos, publishing, writing, and more.

If you are not sure how to create a workshop, attend some in your genre/topic. This will give you some ideas about how to organize a workshop and how to handle yourself as the presenter.

Use your book as a guide to creating a workshop. List the things that your customers typically ask about. Include this information in your workshop or seminar outline.

Present your program through a local college, art center, library system, senior center, corporation, spa/resort or other venue. Or organize your seminar completely on your own by locating a place to have it, arranging for the tables, chairs, food, etc., and doing all of the publicity. I've presented workshops at preorganized conferences, at the local college, in reserved rooms in upscale restaurants, at the local art center, at churches, and in people's homes.

Locate conferences in your genre/topic here:

http://shawguides.com
www.allconferences.com
www.bvents.com

Take Your Book to the Show

There are trade shows geared toward just about every industry you can imagine. There are also shows, fairs, and festivals for the public. If you have a book on hood ornaments for vintage cars, you'll want to exhibit it at car shows. Display your book series on etiquette at gift shows. A book on floral creations or flower arranging might be a big hit at a flower or nursery show. My friend who writes about training dogs might find a market for his books at dog shows, trade shows for pet products, and charitable events involving animal humane leagues, for example.

Exhibit your book at book fairs. Some book fairs are rather like trade shows for the book industry and others are public shows. There are numerous book fairs held throughout the country every year. If you belong to a writing/publishing organization, you will most likely be apprised of some of the many book fairs occurring locally and nationwide. There is typically a fee for displaying your book, and you usually have the option of sharing a booth or having your own. Before getting heavily involved in a book fair, attend a few, study the displays, and watch the people.

You'll notice that some people sell books like hotcakes and others take home the books they came with. Usually, the books that sell are those that are pushed. If you're not an assertive or even aggressive salesperson, it will behoove you to find someone who is. Pay them to represent your book at the fair.

A gentleman at one book fair I attended asked every adult who wandered by if they knew a child who liked to read. Many of them walked away with a copy of his book for their child, niece, nephew, or grandchild. He put his children's book into the hands of every child who walked by and many of them talked their parents into purchasing it. While our booth was a co-op effort and there were six or eight other authors selling their own books, this author was the only one who hawked his book in this way, and he was the only one who sold out of his supply of books that day.

I watched a husband-and-wife team work together to sell her book of poetry at the *Los Angeles Times* Festival of Books several years ago. While she relaxed in a chair off to the side, her husband stood in front of the booth asking passersby if they enjoyed poetry. If they responded, he handed them a book and began describing it. He asked them to read a poem. Soon he was escorting the individual to his wife's side, and she was signing the book for the customer. She sold about thirty $15 books that day—way more than anyone else in the booth.

Make your booth stand out from the rest. Decorate it with colorful posters, balloons, or windsocks, for example. Give away bookmarks, stickers, or sell inexpensive book bags. Have a raffle. Draw a name every hour or so and give away a book. Provide a sign-up sheet. Offer your free newsletter or a free e-book, for example. And add the names to your mailing/e-mailing list.

Be lively. I watched my eighteen-year-old granddaughter work a crowd at a skateboard park opening one weekend several years ago. She represented the family sporting goods store at a booth where she sold t-shirts. She had boxes of stickers and candy to give away. This, and her high energy and friendly manner, had people lining up at her booth while those booths around her remained vacant.

Beware of selling from the wrong booth. I've represented SPAWN (Small Publishers, Artists and Writers Network) many times at the *Los Angeles Times* Festival of Books. But one year, SPAWN didn't have a booth, so I agreed to share space with a mystery and children's book writer. While I generally sell numbers of my writing/publishing-related books at the SPAWN booth, the year that I shared a booth, I sold none. Why?

The SPAWN booth attracts many writers and authors who are interested in talking to us about publishing. Many of them are also in the market for books like mine. The banner across the front of the booth I shared advertised mysteries and children's books. And those are the types of books visitors to this booth were seeking.

There doesn't seem to be a reliable online book festival directory currently, so I suggest that you do a Google search by choosing a city or an organization and your choice of season—couple it with the term "book festival" or "book fair" and see if you can locate appropriate book festivals in the regions of your choice.

Sell more books at book festivals by reading this article: "How to Work a Book Festival So it Works for You" at *www.matilijapress. com/articles/promo_bookfestival.htm*

Appear on Radio and TV

Would the topic of your book make good material for radio and television shows? Can you see yourself being interviewed by talk show hosts? Test the possibilities locally as well as nationally.

Promote Books on Radio and TV

Either call or e-mail the producers of local talk shows and other shows where they typically interview guests. Introduce yourself, give a synopsis of your book and your experience in this field, and let them know you are available for an interview. Send an image of your book cover, your extended bio, and if for television, a photo of yourself. Ask if they would like you to send (or deliver) them a copy of your book. Follow through and follow up, and chances are, they will invite you to appear.

It will improve your chances if you provide a theme for your appearance. If the focus of your book is rather straightforward—it's a guide to local hot spots or provides tips for using time-out more successfully with your kids—then the theme for your presentation is probably set. If, on the other hand, your book features techniques for training an unruly dog, you may want to make suggestions for your interview—the three most common behavior problems with a dog and how to overcome them. It's always a good idea to give your interview a local flavor by providing local resources or mentioning local companies or services relating to your topic.

To get national exposure, research radio and television stations through *Literary Marketplace* and *Gale's Directory of Publications and Broadcast Media.* Also consider purchasing *Radio-TV Interview Report* (215-259-1070). Radio and television producers use this volume to locate interesting personalities and topics for their shows. You can be listed for $200–$700. Also get listed with Guest Finder at *www.guestfinder.com* ($249/year).

You don't have to travel in order to be interviewed for radio. You can do these interviews by phone from your office, kitchen, or hot tub. In fact, I did one in my robe once. (It was 6:00 a.m., for heaven's sakes.) I do recommend dressing for an interview, however, even if it's over the phone, because I believe that you will come across as being more professional when you feel and look more professional.

Learn more about how to get radio interviews and how to handle yourself once you do by reading Francine Silverman's book, *Talk Radio for Authors, Getting Interviews Across the US and Canada.* This $75 book is $67.50 when purchased from Silverman's website: *www.talkradioadvocate.com.* Or consider purchasing *The Radio Book.* It lists over 14,000 stations. Purchase it at a reduced rate of $89.95 at *www.theradiobook.com.*

Gerri Helms is the author of *Trust God and Buy Broccoli; A Spiritual Approach to Weight Loss.* She took to radio as a method of promoting her book right away. She says, "I was invited to be a guest on a local AM radio station and just loved it. My nephew works for a station in Dallas and was able to get me a few gigs on some highly exposed morning shows in California and Texas. Discovering Fran Silverman (who books authors for radio shows) opened the door to regular guest spots."

Do radio appearances sell books? According to Helms, "Whenever I do a show, I have a little flurry of book sales on my website." And she doesn't sit quietly and wait for opportunities to appear. She says, "While Fran finds most of them for me, I also solicit shows myself when I see that someone has a blog-radio show where I am a good fit. There's a website that sends me frequent requests for guests (*www.radioguestlist.com*). I also network with other life and health coaches who share shows that have benefitted them."

What would she recommend to others who want to promote their books through radio? "I find it is helpful to send a copy of my book to the show host so they can ask me questions about the book. I have one copy that is my radio copy with tabs on my favorite pages or quotes that make for good conversation."

She also suggests that you use Facebook, Twitter, and your blog and/or newsletter to announce when you'll be on the shows.

Guidelines for Your Radio Interview

Most hosts appreciate it when you give them a copy of your book, your bio, a couple of reviews, and some potential questions for them to ask you.

Be prepared with notes representing points you want to cover. I generally use sticky tabs on key pages in the book for quick reference. I might label the sticky tabs, "Book Trailers," "Book Reviews," "Book Signings," and so forth.

Prepare physically and mentally for a ten-minute to an hour radio interview. For example:

- Choose a quiet room for the interview.
- Use a landline—it is way more reliable than a cell phone.
- Turn off call waiting.
- Put dogs out and close any open windows to muffle the sound of lawn mowers, power tools, motorcycles, and trucks driving by.
- Stand up or sit tall while involved in a telephone/radio interview. Your voice will carry better and sound more full of life.
- Put some energy into your voice. One way to do this is to have a sense of confidence and excitement about your topic.
- Do more than just answer questions. Be informative and helpful.
- Avoid sounding like a commercial.

Generally, the show host will guide you through the interview by asking questions that, perhaps, you have provided. But be prepared for anything. Once, when I was preparing for a one-hour radio spot later that morning, I e-mailed the host just to make sure we were on schedule. He said, "Yes. Now here is the agenda. You call in and, when you hear the click, that is your cue to start talking. After thirty-five minutes, you can ask for questions. The show will end at precisely 11:30 a.m."

"What?" I couldn't believe my eyes. There would be no host? I was on my own—I would have to speak on behalf of my book for a solid hour? And I had a mere forty-five minutes to prepare.

What did I do? I spent fifteen minutes meditating—calming myself down while visualizing a smooth presentation. And the next thirty minutes were devoted to organizing my notes.

Naturally, there were some anxious moments leading up to the show, but a shift in consciousness and perspective helped me to glide right through the show without a hitch.

Host Your Own Show

If you have a good presentation personality and if you love performing, consider creating your own radio or television show around the theme of your book. Research local radio stations and come up with an idea that would improve the quality of their offerings. Then write a succinct proposal to present to the program director.

Could you spend an hour or two each week responding to questions about using herbal remedies, for example? This exposure would certainly generate sales for a book on growing herbs. A segment featuring sports history trivia would surely spark interest in a book on that subject. Promote your book on African violets through a radio show all about houseplants.

If you can't get in on the regular radio/TV networks, become involved with public radio or TV stations.

One author I know began her radio career by offering a brief segment for a writing show airing on public radio. Each week, she'd ask a literary question, and the first person in radio-land to come up with the right answer won a copy of her book. It wasn't long before this author had her own show. And she continued giving away copies of her book—and why not? Each time she ran a contest, she got to publicize her book on the air. Presumably, with each free give-away copy, she gained several sales.

Sell Your Book through Retail Stores

Having books in chain bookstores throughout the United States is the goal for most American authors and publishers. But how do you go about getting your book accepted? And what can you do to keep your book in the stores?

As authors, we should also ask ourselves, is this actually a reasonable goal? Are bookstores the best place to sell books these days? Not unless the author has developed an aggressive marketing plan. It is up to the author or publisher to bring customers to the bookstores to purchase your book. If you think this can be accomplished, here are some tips for getting your book accepted.

Place Your Book in Bookstores

In order to break into chain bookstores, first check their websites to find out if they offer guidelines for submitting your book for consideration. If not, e-mail, write, or call to ask for this information. To get the name, number, and address for acquisitions, refer to *www.bookstores-guide.com*.

Most major bookstores buy their books through distributors. Generally, they purchase books from independent publishers only when a customer places a special order and only if your book is in the bookstore's database. Most booksellers refer to the *Books in Print* database. You can sign up to have your book included for free by filling out an Advanced Book Information (ABI) form obtained at the

R.R. Bowker site *www.bowkerlink.com*. With every rule, however, there are exceptions.

Some large chain stores will carry books by local authors. Approach the buyer at the stores near you and inquire about their policies.

Some large bookstores have warehouse programs. This means that they will warehouse a few copies of your books so they have them in stock should they receive an order. But your book must qualify.

Independent bookstores are generally small-publisher/author friendly. Visit those in your area, show the manager your book, and ask if they will stock it. Contact specialty bookstores throughout the United States. When I came out with the luau book, I bought a mailing list of bookstores that specialize in cookbooks. Several of them purchased copies of my luau book. There are also physical bookstores that specialize in books on cats, law, business, religion, women's issues, etc., and those that specialize only in metaphysical books, fiction, mysteries, books for children, and books of poetry, for example. Of course, there are online bookstores specializing in virtually every theme and genre.

Once your book has been accepted into a bookstore, develop and maintain a good rapport with the bookstore manager along with a good business sense.

- Check on their supply of your books regularly.
- Make deliveries promptly.
- Keep accurate records.
- Use invoices printed with your company name, address, and phone number.
- Stay on top of the account. Some small bookstores need occasional nudging to pay their bills.

Contact information for major bookstores:

Barnes and Noble author/publisher information: *www.barnesand-noble.com/help/cds2.asp?PID=8148* or go to *www.barnesandnoble.*

com. Scroll down, look under B&N services, and click on "Author and Publisher Guidelines."

Borders Books: *http://www.borders.com/online/store/BGIView_ publishersartists* or go to *www.borders.com.* Scroll down and click on "About Us" and then "Publishers and Artists."

When doing business directly with a bookseller, they typically want a 40 percent discount on the books they accept for sale. In other words, if your book sells for $10, the bookstore will pay you $6 each. In this time of high competition for the author and low sales for the bookseller, there are some creative options being presented. One independent bookseller in our community now wants 50 percent of the selling price from local authors.

Ideally, you would get paid at the time of delivery or, at least, within thirty days of the bookstore receiving a shipment But the reality is that most booksellers dealing with individual authors/ publishers want a consignment agreement—they'll pay you when the books sell (which generally means within sixty or ninety days after the sale).

While the independent bookseller will sometimes agree to order copies of your book from you, chain bookstores and many *indies* prefer making their purchases through distributors and wholesalers. (Read more about working with distributors and wholesalers below in this chapter.)

Expect to pay postage when sending a shipment of books to a bookseller unless they have placed a special order for a customer. Typically, they will charge the customer for shipping, so you can charge the bookseller.

Seek Out Appropriate Specialty Stores

Many books are conducive to sales in specialty stores. I'm speaking of gift shops, stationery stores, feed stores, pet stores, jewelry stores, auto supply shops, and others. Two local brothers wrote a book designed to help children deal with diabetes, and it sold well through local pharmacies. A book of inspirational poems might be a welcome item in a hospital gift shop. Debbie Puente's book on crème brûlée sold at kitchen stores. My luau book sold through barbecue stores. A book on some aspect of aviation or parachuting would surely be accepted for sale in small airports throughout the United States. I'd pitch a book on how to create curb appeal when selling a home through real estate offices.

It doesn't take a lot of imagination to match your book with interesting specialty stores. For example, I sold my local history book in the museum gift shop, from the Board of Realty office, and in busy tourist shops downtown. Tweed Scott sells his book, *Texas in Her Own Words*, at the Alamo. Dena Harris, however, has gone beyond creative and even logic when it comes to venues for her book, *Lessons in Stalking: Adjusting to Life With Cats*. She says, "The first year my book was published, I took it to the Cat Fancier's Association National Convention. There were huge halls filled with cat lovers. I figured I'd clean up. Not so much. I think I sold six books. The problem is that my book was just one of many cat items. Alternatively, when I place my book in unexpected places such as art galleries, spas, and furniture stores, it gets much more attention."

But what about selling fiction in nontraditional outlets? Carolyn Howard-Johnson reveals some of the places where she sold her novel, *This Is the Place*, "Because the story was set in Utah, this made it suitable for souvenir shops in the Intermountain West. It deals with tolerance. That made it suitable for kind of hippy/liberal coffee shops and Internet cafes. It was based on family journals. That made it suitable for shops in and around the Mormon temple that cater to genealogists and journalers." She also sold it in the Autry Museum of Western History in Los Angeles and other shops that cater to history buffs.

Arrange for Point of Purchase Displays

If you know of a specialty store where you could conceivably sell copies of your book, but they don't typically sell books, offer to provide a point of purchase display for your books. Here are a few sites where you can order book display racks.

www.bookdisplays.com
www.displays2go.com
www.cardboarddisplays.com

Sign With a Distributor/Wholesaler

If you have been published by a traditional royalty publisher, you don't have to deal with distributors or distribution. Your publisher will handle this. But if you have self-published (established your own publishing company), you'll want to become familiar with the process of distribution.

Most bookstores today rely on distributors and wholesalers to furnish them books, because booksellers prefer having only a few invoices to pay each month rather than hundreds from individual publishers. But, having a publisher does not relieve you of your marketing duties and neither does having a distributor or wholesaler. The author is still responsible for promoting his or her book. As Dan Poynter says in his book *The Self-Publishing Manual*, "Distributors replace part of your shipping department, but you must always do the marketing yourself."

While many distributors have sales reps in the field selling books to bookstores, wholesalers only provide books when the bookstore orders them for their customers. This means that you have to reach their customers through your marketing efforts.

Many distributors specialize. Some are regional suppliers, others only handle books in certain areas of interest: spiritual, religion, health, or juvenile, for example.

Not every distributor will accept every book. There is usually a screening process. Before saying yes to your book, a distributor may want to know what you're doing to promote it. They may ask for a sales history. Sometimes a distributor or wholesaler won't take your book until it has proven itself in the marketplace. Some distributors want an exclusive contract. My Hawaiian distributor for the luau book, for example, wanted exclusivity in the Hawaiian Islands.

Distributors don't work for free. They require a percentage of the sales, leaving you (the publisher) anywhere from 32 to 45 percent of the retail price. (You can sometimes negotiate a larger percentage for yourself if the wholesaler or distributor doesn't warehouse your books.) Once you've signed with a distributor, they may ask you to pay for inclusion in their catalog. You will also pay shipping to the distributor/wholesaler.

Some authors refuse to pay the price. They'd rather go it alone. I believe, however, that wholesalers and distributors can make a difference in your bottom line. Baker and Taylor ordered over 250 copies of my luau book one year. My profit on those books wasn't as much as on the copies I sold myself. But I have to wonder if the bookstores and libraries would have bothered ordering those books directly from me.

My regional Hawaiian distributor ordered 1,200 luau books over a two-year period, when they were distributing it. That's about fifty books per month that I would not have sold without them. As an aside, these figures prompted a publisher of Hawaiian books to issue me a contract for the luau book. They published the third edition.

Find listings for distributors and wholesalers in *Literary Market Place*. If you're not sure which distributor to go with, contact publishers of books similar to yours and ask who distributes their books.

What's the difference between a distributor and a wholesaler? Generally, the distributor stocks books, and some of them have reps who show it around to their accounts. A wholesaler typically orders books on an as-need basis.

You may be asked to pay a processing fee of around $100 before getting started with a wholesaler or distributor. As with any company or entity you contemplate doing business with, read the contract. Run it by a publishing or intellectual properties attorney and, if you want to make a side agreement with this company, do so in writing.

These are the two most prominent wholesalers of books in the United States:

Baker and Taylor, Inc.
www.btol.com btinfo@btol.com

1-800-775-1800
Ingram Book Company
www.ingrambook.com
One Ingram Blvd.
La Vergne, TN 37068
Online directories of distributors:
www.ibpa-online.org/pubresources/distribute.aspx
www.publishersglobal.com. (Includes distributors as well as publishers worldwide.)
www.bookmarket.com/distributors.htm
http://www.morganprinting.org/Resources1.html (Includes fulfillment services.)

Engage a Fulfillment Company

A fulfillment company warehouses and ships your books. The fee and percentage depend on the nature of the services you require, the number of books involved, and so forth.

As with any contract agreement, understand and approve of it before you sign it. I know an author who sat down with a well-known fulfillment and distribution company representative to discuss some particulars of their agreement, which were very important to this author. The rep made some promises, and the author believed them. However, these things were not in the contract, and these important promises were never fulfilled. This author ended up losing $3,000 and selling zero books in the process.

Directories of fulfillment services:
http://www.bookmarket.com/4.htm
http://www.morganprinting.org/Resources1.html (Includes book distributors/wholesalers.)

Protect Yourself from Publishing Scams

As one publishing professional pointed out recently, because there is so much more need for publishing services and because so many authors are making emotional instead of informed decisions, there are more scammers being lured into the folds of this industry. They come in the form of distribution and fulfillment companies, literary agents, publishers, pay-to-publish companies, book shepherds, editors, and others.

Use the warning sites designed for writers and authors before making a final decision anytime there is a contract presented and money will change hands. Do a Google search using keywords "warning" and the name of the company. Or visit these warning sites specifically designed for authors:

www.anotherealm.com/prededitors
www.todayswriting.com/poetry-scams.html
www.writersweekly.com/whispers_and_warnings.php
www.sfwa.org/for-athors/writer-beware

Get Creative with Book Promotion

There are as many book promotion ideas and activities as there are authors. While it is important to consider your comfort zone when designing a marketing plan, it is equally necessary to try new things. Let this chapter inspire you to get creative.

Sell Books for Conference Goodie Bags

Almost every type of conference, from writers' conferences to those focusing on dogs, librarians, fitness, business management, travel, advertising, education, paranormal, law, and so forth, involve goodie bags. Advertisers donate all sorts of products as well as things with logos—pens, tee shirts, bookmarks, notepads, and so forth. It isn't uncommon for conference attendees to find books in their goodie bags.

Use some of the more popular conference directories (listed below) to locate appropriate conferences. Contact the directors and see if you can make a deal to have your book included in their goodie bags.

Tip: Expect to give discounts of from 20 to 65 percent, depending on the number of books they require. If you aren't making a profit on the deal, I would turn it down—unless you believe that the exposure will lead to greater sales.

http://shawguides.com
www.allconferences.com
www.bvents.com

Design and Teach Courses Related to Your Topic or Genre

If you're qualified, teach online courses or real-time workshops on your book's topic. I offer online courses on article writing, book promotion, self-publishing, writing a book proposal, memoir writing, and self-editing. The concept of an online course is fairly simple, actually. I write the lectures and develop the assignments for my six- or eight-week courses—sending students a lecture and an assignment each week. I then work with students on their projects as they complete their assignments by offering feedback, guidance, and editing help. I teach the courses on demand, meaning that anyone can sign up at anytime. I'll run the course for one student or several.

I see courses offered for a wide range of fees. I charge $125 to $200, depending on the course. Read "How an online course works" here: *www.matilijapress.com/course_howwork.htm*

What are the benefits of presenting an online course or presenting live workshops? These add-on services afford greater exposure for you and your book. If you charge for the course, you are making a little extra money. Your students are highly apt to purchase copies of your book. And the more services you offer, the more publicity you can reasonably get and the more credibility you will earn.

If you're not sure how to proceed with this idea, consider purchasing the lesson plans of others who are teaching similar courses. This might help you to develop a unique and useful course of your own.

Offer Your Book as a Prize

There are many ways to do this. Run a contest at your site and use your book as the prize. This is especially successful when your book is a hefty price—$30 or more. Offer your book free to the first one who answers your question of the week in your blog. Announce your contest in appropriate newsletters and magazines in order to bring people to your website.

I've donated my books as prizes for other contests. Scour the Internet for suitable contests and offer your book to the organizers. What are the benefits? Your book will be featured at the contest site for a period of time before and after the contest. It will be mentioned in any promo going out about the contest. You can use this opportunity to place announcements about the contest in your club and organization publications as well.

Tap into a Specialty Market

While you're eager to get your book placed in traditional bookstores, you may actually sell more copies through specialty markets. Doctors, psychologists, and funeral directors might buy copies of your book on healthy grieving to give to their clients and patients, for example. This book would also sell in hospital gift shops.

Is your book conducive to an audience outside of the general public, college students, for example, military families, seniors, baby boomers, home owners? If so, find ways to address this market.

Some books make great gift items. And where do we go to purchase gifts? If we are shopping for someone who likes remote control airplanes, we go to a hobby shop. And this might be a good place for your book on flying remote control airplanes. When you need a gift for someone who loves sports, you probably visit a sporting goods store. What better place for a book featuring the world's greatest sportscasters?

Send Your Book to School

If your book has educational aspects for children, consider offering it to school districts nationwide. Betty Louise Middleton Britton's book on the early Spanish days in California is geared toward fourth and fifth grade students because, in this state, that's when they study California history. Consequently, some of her best customers are California school districts.

My Ojai history book is often used by local teachers. First, it is in virtually every school library in the Ojai School District. Secondly, fourth and fifth grade teachers in private and public schools in this community use it in their curriculum at some point during the year. One high school teacher uses it as a text for a class of at-risk teens. She discovered that these students could relate more easily to local history than to the history of faraway places.

If it is a children's book that teaches a character value, consider having it accepted in the Character Counts program. This program operates in hundreds of school districts throughout the nation, and the organization is always seeking good books to recommend to participating teachers. *www.charactercounts.org.*

If your print book is suitable for students at any level, you might consider creating an e-book version. Sooner or later many states will shift from the more bulky, relatively disposable, expensive hardcopy book to e-book formats. Whether you're pitching a print book or an e-book, start by seeing if you can engage one of the wholesalers or distributors for the education market such as American Reading Company, AKJ Books, Books4School, or the Booksource. If you are already involved with Baker and Taylor, you might want to approach them about the idea of targeting your book for the education market. Get a list of distributors and wholesalers for schools at *www.edupaperback.org/distributors.cfm.*

Next, contact individual school districts and speak with the librarian or the person in charge of curriculum or acquisitions. Start your campaign near home. Listen to the feedback and information you get from the directors at your local district. And then devise a plan to take your book on the road either virtually or actually.

Some professionals say that schools are not a very good market for books, but that students are. If you want to get speaking opportunities at the grammar school level, start by calling the principal of the individual school. Let him or her refer you to the librarian or media specialist (usually the same person). According to Diana Zimmerman, who successfully markets her book to students at the grammar school level (see sidebar below), "Sometimes these people are very hard to get online, so persistence is key."

Directory of school districts throughout the United States: *www.districtbug.org.*

If the students like your book, the librarian will generally order copies for their library.

Perhaps your book is more suited to the college student. One way to get your book noticed at this level is to contact college and university librarians: *http://lists.webjunction.org/libweb/Academic_CA.html*. If your book has an academic appeal, contact appropriate professors and ask if you can send them a sample copy. If the book is already in their library, suggest that they check it out. Locate U.S. colleges and universities here: *www.50states.com/college*. Even if your book isn't destined to be a textbook, it may be appropriate for school libraries or college bookstores. For a directory of colleges and universities: *www.braintrack.com*

Diana Zimmerman, the author of a young adult fantasy, *Kandide and the Secret of the Mists*, thought long and hard about her marketing plan before launching out on a bookselling mission. She says, "I realized that the only way to get attention was to create it. But what to do? Where to go? That's when I decided to start where my readers are—schools."

She hired someone to help her get into the schools. And this was no easy task. As Zimmerman says, "Many principals and librarians did not want an unknown author. But, as with all things, perseverance prevailed." And she has since developed a good relationship with schoolteachers and librarians throughout the states. "They love *Kandide* because it is not dark, but packed with action, and I provide a strong anti-bullying/self-esteem, motivational message."

According to Zimmerman, "I can speak at up to twenty schools in a week. That's four a day. It's a lot of work, but it's well worth it. To date, she says, over 30,000 schoolkids all over the country have experienced *Kandide*." She describes her marketing plan. "I speak at the school to as many kids as possible, generally third through fifth grades. Then I give out coupons for the kids to get a free bookmark when they come to Barnes and Noble that evening, where I've arranged to do a book signing."

Make News

Don't sit back and wait for a reason to seek publicity. Go out and do something newsworthy. If your book is on dog training, you know that a well-trained dog is more desirable than an unruly dog. So, help abandoned dogs find homes by offering to teach volunteers at local shelters to work with the dogs that come in for adoption. And be sure to tell the press about what you're doing. This activity should rate a story in your county newspaper as well as other newspapers across the United States. If the adoption rate goes up because of your efforts, this is an even better story. In this case, consider approaching the editors of dog magazines, for example, and suggest a story. Be sure to mention your book during the interview.

Maybe you've written a novel featuring a homeless family. Make news by spearheading an effort to find housing for a local homeless family, a job for a homeless person, or start a hot meals program for the homeless. I read about a young woman once who made sandwiches and delivered them to the homeless every Sunday afternoon. While her charitable effort is localized, the story hit the national news. She wasn't an author—but imagine if she was. This would have been great publicity for her book.

If you've written a children's book, participate in story time at libraries throughout your state and precede these events with news releases to newspapers. A book on hiking might get extra press if you were to organize a charity hike, monthly senior hikes, or hikes for special-needs students, for example.

I presented a luau for one hundred people once and invited the press. This made a wonderful story with great pictures for a large spread in our county newspaper—a great way to publicize my luau book.

Engage in Creative Internet Marketing

One reason why so many more people are writing books these days is because of easy access to their readers. Most authors and publishers are promoting their books through the Internet, and some of them do so exclusively. While you'll discover basic and even advanced Internet marketing tips and ideas throughout this book, here are a few of the more creative ones. And they're free.

Join "groups" and "lists" related to the theme/genre of your book and then participate. You'll meet potential customers and connect with other professionals in your field. (Read more about this in chapter eight.)

Register with services such as HARO (Help a Reporter Out): *www.helpareporter.com*. Every morning and afternoon, you will receive e-mail listings from journalists seeking assistance with articles and so forth. If you have the experience or expertise to respond to certain requests, this could result in great magazine and newspaper publicity for your book.

Sign up to receive Google Alerts: *www.google.com/alerts*. Use keywords related to your book's theme/genre and you will be alerted when someone posts an article, blog, or something else related to your topic. Follow the links and comment where applicable.

Organize a virtual author tour or engage a professional to do this for you. John Kremer lists nearly fifty resources for authors who are seeking Internet publicity opportunities, such as virtual tours: *http:// www.bookmarket.com/blogtours.htm*. A virtual tour might include getting recognition through blogs related to the theme or genre of your book, getting your book reviewed, submitting articles to sites and e-newsletters, being interviewed for online broadcasts and podcasts, being featured at social media sites, and more.

Use Your Writing Skills

You are a writer; why not promote your book using your God-given talents? Following are six ways to do this:

Write Magazine Articles

Write informative, useful articles for magazines or short stories in your book's genre. How will this activity serve to promote your book? By getting your stories published, you are creating a following—readers who appreciate your writing and who, because of this, will probably purchase your novel.

By landing article-writing assignments in appropriate magazines and newsletters, you will attract attention from your target audience. You will continue to build on your credibility as an expert in your field. And you will get added exposure for your book.

Start by listing possible topics. If your book features modern-day inventors, for example, write a story about women inventors for a women's magazine. You might offer a piece on inventors of things related to communications technology for a computer, high-tech or science magazine. An article about what it takes to get a patent might grab the attention of a general interest magazine editor.

There may be hundreds of article ideas in your nonfiction book and, if you are a novelist, you should be able to write several hundred short stories over time to submit to magazines.

Study the magazines for which you want to write. Find magazines in large bookstores, magazine outlets, and listed in *Writer's Market*. This volume also gives guidelines for submitting articles to magazines.

Always, always study each magazine's specific guidelines for writers before submitting. Never rely solely on the contact information and guidelines listed in *Writer's Market*. (Find submission guidelines at the publication's website or call or e-mail asking for a copy.)

There are two excellent online magazine databases: *www.writersmarket.com* and *www.woodenhorsepub.com*. Both charge a fee. If you're serious about submitting articles and stories, I recommend that you pay the fee for at least one of these databases.

I've sold many articles promoting *The Mainland Luau*. I wrote one for *Reunions Magazine* featuring how to present a luau at a family reunion. *National Barbecue News* bought my piece on various ways to roast a whole pig. Several regional magazines published my articles on presenting a backyard luau.

I sold numerous articles designed to promote my long-distance grandparenting book. They were published in religious, regional, parenting, spiritual, association, and general publications.

I consistently submit articles on writing and publishing to dozens of magazines and newsletters in order to promote my books on writing and publishing.

Not only is this a good way to get exposure for your book and drum up sales, you can also get paid for your articles. Rates vary from magazine to magazine. You might earn as much as $2,000 for an article or as little as $50. Of course, some magazines and newsletters don't pay at all. But even if you don't get a check for a submission, if it's published, you've received great exposure.

Meagan Francis was rather surprised to discover how far a published article could take an author along the bumpy book marketing road. She says, "The timing seemed especially right in the late summer / early fall of 2008 for an article on the topic of my book, *Table for Eight: Raising a Large Family in a Small-Family World*." So she submitted an opinion piece to the *Christian Science Monitor*. They published it, and things really started happening for Francis. She explains, "The essay was great publicity. I wound up getting a lot of reader e-mail and then other opportunities started rolling in."

According to Francis, "I was featured in a *New York Times* story on big families (on the front page of the Sunday Styles section). I was on the *John and Ken* radio show in Los Angeles, was interviewed for the *Chicago Sun Times,* and appeared on the Dr. Nancy Snyderman show on MSNBC among other things."

Certainly, she recommends article writing as a way to gain more exposure for your book. She says, "My next book, *The Happiest Mom: 10 Secrets to Enjoying Motherhood,* comes out in April of 2011, and I definitely plan to make writing part of my publicity mix. I think it is a really effective way to get your name, opinion and book title in front of people."

Get Your Articles Published on the Web

Like it or not, the web pretty much rules. If we want information, we turn to our computers. So it would behoove you to spread some of your articles around the Internet. Find out where your readers or folks interested in the topic of your book do their research or their searches on this topic and post some of your articles there.

If you know of major sites within your niche, check to see if they post articles. If so, read their submission guidelines and consider contributing appropriate articles. Do your own search to locate other suitable websites that publish articles on the topic of your book. And then start seeking out directories within your niche. Using directories to locate promotional opportunities is a huge time-saver. Well, it saves you time when it comes to the initial search, but you may actually spend more time visiting the huge number of sites you locate in each directory and writing and submitting articles. And that's a good thing!

When doing a search for directories, type in "directory + your niche topic." For example, "directory of gardening sites," "parenting site directory," "directory of private school sites," "cat sites, "bird-watching sites," "freshwater aquarium sites," "real estate sites," etc. When I tested this activity out using "gardening," I located several directory sites. One, in particular, had twenty-two links including "publications," "florists," "greenhouses," and "water gardening."

I did a search for "business management site directories" and found one with forty-five links to sites focused on accounting, e-commerce, law, writing and editing, transportation, small business, and so forth.

Publish a Newsletter

Promote your books through a monthly e-mail or snail mail newsletter. Many e-mail newsletters are free to subscribers.

Newsletters have been informing readers rather inexpensively for a long time. Even insurance companies, hospitals, utility companies, and investment companies send newsletters to their customers.

If you want to publish a newsletter, weigh the time commitment against the benefits. If you have one book to sell, the benefits of producing a free newsletter probably isn't that great for you. If you frequently produce new books and other related material, courses, workshops, etc., it may be worth your while to use this as a means of spreading the word to your audience.

A newsletter is even more beneficial to you if you're running a business related to your book. If you train dogs, for example, and sell merchandise along with a training manual, a newsletter might be a good idea. Maybe you buy and sell vintage car parts. The contacts you can make through a newsletter might far exceed any inconvenience. If you offer services as well as products, you could definitely gain from a newsletter.

Do not produce a newsletter simply as a means to sell books. Your intention should be to give something of value to your customers while positioning yourself as an expert in your field or niche.

Before starting a newsletter, study other newsletters. Note the things you like and dislike about them. Talk to people interested in your topic and ask what they would like to read in a newsletter. Maybe they can tell you what's missing in other publications. Read magazines on your topic for column and content ideas.

Ideally, you would provide news or facts of interest to your particular audience, share new research findings, introduce new movers and shakers in the industry or genre, give the particulars of a contest you're running, and of course, offer a spiel on your services, book, and other material you have for sale.

To get started, check out the following:
www.thesitewizard.com/archive/newsletter.shtml
www.enewsletterpro.com
www.newsletterease.com.

Many authors produce newsletters in order to maintain a connection with their audiences. Karon Korp, author of *Remembering Our Spiritual Journey Home: The 12 Keys for Awakening the Memory of Who You Are and Why You Are Here,* describes hers, "It's a monthly compilation of important elements for spiritual growth and personal development with added emphasis on energies and themes affecting our lives. I include regular columns, recommended websites/practices/programs and featured products from my online store." She says, "The goal is to enlighten people and provide them with tools and information they may not have access to from other sources."

She uses Constant Contact to distribute her monthly newsletter. How does the newsletter tie into book promotion? "Frequently, I will quote portions from my book or advertise a book special that directs readers to my website." She reminds other authors, "It is not the book you are selling, but *you.* Authors are better served focusing on building an audience and providing information that serves their readers. The key is to be consistent in your delivery with fresh new topics of interest and creative ways to get yourself out there in front of people."

Develop a Column

Design a newspaper or magazine column related to your topic. What do you gain when you reach out in this way? Additional credibility in your field and the potential to sell more books.

This experience might also lead to more published books. Just imagine how much new information you'll discover when you're required to come up with a fresh column idea each week or month.

If your book topic lends itself well to a column, contact appropriate magazine and newspaper editors with your ideas. You could easily develop a column from the following subjects: gardening, cooking, home decorating, sports, music, parenting, physical fitness/health, herbal remedies, seniors/retirement, pet care, automobiles, business, poetry, and computers.

There are a variety of types of column types:

- Essay (you share your thoughts and perspective on world events, education, politics, or?).
- How-to (you teach aspects of some activity—cooking, gardening, parenting, crafts, healthy living, for example).
- Reporting (you write about what's happening in sports, world events, local schools, politics, etc.).
- Theme (seniors, pets, book reviews, ghosts/spirits, art . . .).
- Informative (medical, hiking, real estate, automotive).
- Advice (relationships, health and fitness, spirituality, religion, diet . . .).

How do you land a column? Here are some ideas:
- Look for a need. What is missing from your local newspaper or your favorite magazine, e-zine, or website that you could provide?
- List column ideas. Can you come up with enough ideas to fill your column for the next several months? If you can't list a year's worth of column ideas (for a monthly column) or three months' worth (for a weekly column), you might want to consider another theme.
- Create some sample columns. Go out and interview a few people or write a few columns and then present your idea and the examples to the editor.

Tips:
- A new publication might be more open to column ideas. They are also more apt to close.

- Consider the audience before pitching your idea. If you're writing for a regional publication, make sure that your column always has a local flavor. If it is a regional magazine on parenting, then your audience is interested in parenting issues and activities, events, services occurring/rendered locally. If it is a national health magazine, your focus should be aspects of health for all Americans.
- Mix it up. It's your column and sometimes you're given quite a bit of leeway. If so, you might write about your experiences in this theme or topic, conduct an occasional interview (with experts and with regular citizens), review related products, report on extreme happenings and occurrences within the realm of your theme topic, express your thoughts on the topic, and so forth.

Establish Your Own Blog

Set up a blog designed around the theme/topic of your book. A blog is a web log—sort of like a journal or diary. You can make it anything you want it to be. You can teach, inform, share, or entertain. You can speak your piece, give strong advice, offer resources and solutions, or simply have fun with it. The point of a blog is to communicate regularly with your audience, develop a rapport with them, and keep them coming back to find out what, of interest and value, you have to share each day.

We've all heard of publishers issuing contracts to bloggers that produce interesting content. That's right—publishers will pursue those with publishable blogs. And bloggers with interesting and useful posts are often invited to be interviewed, appear on radio/TV shows, write articles, etc., based on their expertise.

I have two blog sites. One is related to *Catscapades*, my book of cat stories. The other is a writing and publishing blog. I add to this blog every single day even when I am traveling. Yes, you can post blog entries from anyplace where you have an Internet connection.

A key to building a following for your blog is to continually publish something of value related to the theme or genre of your book. You have free rein with your blog. If you want to be read, however, you'd better fulfill the needs and desires of your audience. It can be lonely out there in blogger-land when you keep writing/posting and nothing is coming back in your direction—the world around you is silent.

As writers, we want to be read. For the majority of us, that's why we write. While we can track visitors to our sites and our blogs, a chart just isn't the same as receiving personal comments.

Here's what I recommend:

- Add new blog entries regularly—at least once a week and preferably every day.
- Offer information, breaking news, resources, and your perspective on issues pertinent to your field, topic, or genre.
- Look at your blog as you would a magazine seeking articles—consider writing profile or interview pieces, Q and A posts, rants (we all enjoy reading a good rant), book or product review, and, my favorite, the instructional post.
- Post current news items and refer to well-known people involved in your topic or genre and you may begin to acquire a more varied following.
- Note where you'll be speaking or signing next, online classes you'll be teaching, and publications where your book has been reviewed, etc.
- Promote your book and/or services in each and every blog entry, even if it's just a brief reminder.
- Encourage dialogue. Use the comments function of your blog. Promote comments by bringing up controversial issues, launching contests, and presenting challenges.
- Provide freebies and discounts.
- Advertise your blog in your bio when you submit articles for publication, on your Facebook and Twitter pages as well as on your business cards, brochures, etc.
- Make it easy for your website visitors to locate the link to your blog.

Many of your blog topics can be expanded or tweaked into articles for magazines and e-zines in your book's topic or genre.

You may wonder, can you create a blog that promotes your novel? Certainly. Here are some ideas:

- Reveal excerpts from your story.
- Discuss the process of writing fiction.
- Share some of your insights with regard to your story or writing or fiction, in general.
- Let your characters drive your blog—write side stories around your characters or bring up important issues and life situations and discuss how your characters would handle them. I know of a blog that is written by a cat.
- Write new short stories for your blog at least occasionally.

Children's book authors might find it more challenging to promote their books through blogs. You can blog about the children's book industry, illiteracy, library use for children, various reading programs in libraries and schools throughout the United States. Be creative. Study similar blogs to get ideas for yours.

Here are some of the more popular blog programs and, at least, some of them are *free.*

www.Blosxom.com
http://Nucleuscms.org
www.MovableType/org
http://WordPress.org

Get Your Blog Site Listed

Establishing a blog is only the first step. Now you must advertise it. One way, of course, is through social media sites. (See chapter eight.) But there's more that you can do. Encourage pings. Pinging is a way to spread the word about your blog. Allow pings and your blog is more apt to appear in many more search engines. Most blog programs provide a list of ping sites you can choose from. You can also sign up with *www.feedburner.com.*

Perhaps you've noticed the RSS feed logo at blog sites. Most likely, you have the option for RSS feed at your site. Be sure to access it so that your blog followers can click on it and subscribe to your blog. Each time you post, your subscribers will be notified. You can use the RSS feed service built into your blog system or subscribe with an outside service such as:

www.feedburner.com

www.feedblitz.com

Many blogs are rated. Do a search and you'll find a list of the top ten blogs for writers, the best culinary blogs, etc. Sometimes the rating is given by an agency or group within that genre/topic. But often, these are presented by an individual blogger. Contact the group or individual and tell them about your blog. Ask them to review several posts and to consider you the next time they list their favorite blog sites.

Be a Guest Blogger

This is something that is often overlooked by authors—the opportunity to be read at established blogs related to your topic or genre.

Sign up for Google Alerts (*www.google.com/alerts*) using key words that will bring up blog sites similar to yours. You'll become aware of many other sites on the theme or genre of your book where you can comment, be a guest blogger, or be interviewed, for example.

Offer to contribute to popular blogs in your expertise. The more exposure you get as an expert on your topic, the more likely you will be noticed by the media.

Locate blogs similar to yours:

www.technorati.com

www.feedster.com

www.blogpulse.com

Become an Expert

Once you have published a book on a certain topic, you are considered an authority. Sure, you will have critics; we all do. But you'll also be held to high standards when it comes to your subject. And it is this proposed expertise that you should emphasize and enhance throughout the process of promoting your book. Use this advantage to your advantage.

Position Yourself as an Expert

Contact freelance writers and authors who write on your topic and let them know that you're available for interviews. Because I am the author of the most comprehensive local history book ever written about this community, I'm known locally as a historian and am frequently asked to comment on an aspect of valley history for newspaper and magazine features. I've been quoted as an expert on some of my other book topics, as well: long-distance grandparenting, youth mentoring, presenting a luau, and journaling. With each quote published, my name and the title of my related book are included, giving me even greater exposure and credibility.

I've been quoted numerous times related to writing, publishing, and book marketing in newsletters, magazine articles, and several books. Some of these opportunities have come about as a result of my many published articles, my active blog site, and of course, my books. But I also keep an eye out for invitations from authors and freelance writers who are seeking quotes from experts in my fields of expertise.

Are you familiar with HARO (Help a Reporter Out)? You can subscribe at *www.helpareporter.com* free. Every day, you will receive a list of current journalistic needs. Respond to those that relate to your expertise and you may be quoted in some prestigious journals and other publications. Here are a few other similar sites:

http://www.reporterconnection.com/press.
http://www.pitchrate.com

Demand Proper Credit

When someone wants to quote you as an expert, make sure that you get proper credit in the article or book where the piece is published. During a newspaper interview once, featuring a story on Ojai, I told the reporter about the latest edition of my Ojai history book, and I showed him a copy. But I forgot to stress that I wanted credit as the author of this book. I assumed that is how I would be credited. Instead, he introduced me as "the Ojai historian," with no mention of the book whatsoever. That was disappointing. Here was a great opportunity for free publicity for my, then, four-month-old revision, and I didn't make sure that it happened.

Don't make this mistake. When it is a face-to-face or telephone interview, state that you want to be credited as the author of such and such book. If it is an e-mail interview or you've commented via e-mail, type out the way you want the credit to read in the published piece.

Keep in mind that the author may have to work this into the article, so keep it brief. If, on the other hand, the credit will be listed aside from the article—in a sidebar or at the end of the piece, for example— then you'll have more room for more information.

Don't fret if the only thing the journalist (or his editor) is able to mention is your book title. If you've done your job correctly—you have a website connected to your book, your book is listed in *Books in Print*, etc.—any potential customer will be able to find you with a quick click of the mouse.

Hang Out Your Shingle

If your book is nonfiction on a topic that you know well, consider hanging out your shingle. I've been writing for publication for over thirty-five years. I am the author of thirty-five books—many of them on writing and publishing. I travel around, giving workshops and other presentations to authors and freelance writers. I write tons of articles on related subjects. I teach live and online courses on various writing/publishing topics. I am considered a professional and an expert. I'm also the executive director of SPAWN and the former president for many years.

Over the years, authors and freelance writers have come to me with questions. At first, I was rather surprised that I had so much information to share. I had numerous authors ask me to help them with their book projects. At first, I didn't feel confident enough to do this, nor was I interested in working on other people's books. I had plenty of my own work to do.

Eventually, however, I began to say yes. And I have enjoyed working on dozens and dozens of book projects in a variety of manners for talented authors for the last twenty years.

My advice to those of you who contemplate becoming a consultant, trainer, teacher, coach, or advisor in your field or genre is to start slow. Find out what others in your field are offering by way of classes, consultations, workshops. Devise your own workshop to discover how much value you can actually share with others. Find out if you are an expert. Do you have meaningful and important knowledge that others could use? Can you teach—do you have what it takes on a personal level? Do students respond to you? Do you enjoy the process of leading others toward whatever measure of success they desire? Then maybe you could be a successful paid mentor, teacher, or coach in your area of expertise.

Quantify Your Expertise at Amazon

One way to help position yourself as an expert before millions of people is by commenting on and reviewing books similar to yours at Amazon.com. Choose books related to the theme/genre of your book. If you're not accustomed to reviewing books, first read the book. Then study the reviews that others wrote about this book. You might also read reviews at other Amazon book pages to get an idea of what to cover in your review. While the maximum review length at Amazon is one thousand words, the ideal is seventy-five to 300 words. As I understand it, adding information about yourself or your book to an Amazon review is now discouraged. But Amazon visitors can learn more about you at your Amazon profile. It is important that you keep your profile up to date with your book titles and contact information. Create or change your Amazon profile here: *www.amazon.com/gp/pdp.*

Some authors review numerous books in their field at Amazon in order to establish greater credibility, visibility, and name recognition.

Author Central has replaced the outdated Amazon Connect. As Amazon says, this is a free service to allow authors to reach more readers, promote books, and help to build a better Amazon bookstore. Here, you can manage your bio, add photographs, and even keep readers updated about your books via a blog. Sign up here: *https://authorcentral.amazon.com/*

Become an Expert through Blogs and Articles

In chapter fifteen, we discuss using your blog and your informative articles to promote your book. In so doing, be sure to always produce meaningful copy that continues to position you as an expert in your field. Use your blog posts and articles to demonstrate what you know about the industry or topic you represent. Strive to teach and share your expertise with your readers. And continue to study, research, and learn so that you always have fresh material to offer.

Remain constant. If you pass along good, useful, and reliable information and resources and do your best to provide assistance to those who contact you for additional support or material, you will build a following and credibility among your readership.

Use Your Expertise by Offering Teleseminars

A teleseminar is a seminar presented by phone to as many as 1,000 people at a time. All you need to get started is a conference call provider and a solid presentation. You advertise a specific date and time for the teleseminar. You can charge for it or offer it for free.

A few days prior to the program, send the call-in number and code to those who signed up for the teleseminar.

In most cases, you can open the lines so everyone has the opportunity to speak and ask questions, or you can mute the incoming lines and proceed with your presentation without interruption.

Most services also offer the capacity to record the teleseminar, so you can offer free or for-a-fee downloads to your website visitors.

Conference call services:

http://xiosoft.com (recommended by another author)
http://www.easycall.net
http://www.conferencecall.com

Let Others Help Promote Your Book

Book promotion can be a mighty lonely activity. You'll find that no one cares about your book as much as you do. And no one can do justice to promoting it like you can. However, authors and publishers cannot successfully promote a book totally alone. It takes a village. Just be sure that you engage the right entities to assist you.

Partner with Online Booksellers Such as Amazon.com

To get your book on Amazon, go to *www.amazon.com*. In the box on the left labeled "Features and Services," click "Advantage Program." As you will see, there is an annual fee of $29.95. Amazon buys books from you at a 55 percent discount and you pay shipping. Some authors choose not to get involved with Amazon. But I bite the bullet and take the hit on the books they sell for the opportunity to display my books at Amazon.com. I figure that the sales made at this site are likely sales that I would not make otherwise. I consider Amazon an extended exposure opportunity. It's a great place to showcase your books, and you can get additional exposure through some of Amazon's extra features. There are the customer reviews posted on your book pages at Amazon, for example, and your author profile in Author Central. (See chapter sixteen.)

There are several other online booksellers you might want to consider; *www.BarnesandNoble.com* and *www.Borders.com* being the most prominent.

How to Keep a Larger Percentage from Online Book Sales

Authors/publishers who print with Lightning Source pay online book-sellers a smaller percentage. Lightning Source is a print-on-demand printer and distributor with a program that offers printing and distribution to online booksellers such as Amazon.com, BarnesandNoble.com, and others around the world. Here's how it works. Instead of sending you a purchase order, the online bookseller issues a purchase order to Lightning Source. They print the book and ship it. This means no storage or shipping fees for the author and no need to send invoices. You simply receive a monthly check from Lightning Source. With this program, instead of 55 percent, as in the Amazon advantage program, Amazon takes only 20 percent.

www.lightningsource.com

Susan Daffron, author of eleven books, has discovered a way to get more from her Amazon.com experience. She has her books printed by Lightning Source (LSI). As she says, "Although many other printers use the same type of short-run printing technology to print books only when ordered, no other company has the distribution advantage Lightning Source does. When you sign up with LSI, you get access to a large distribution network, which includes online booksellers like Amazon.com and bn.com and distributors like Ingram and Baker and Taylor."

A few years ago, Daffron decided to repurpose a lot of her writing in book form, and she researched self-publishing. She says, "I learned that if I went to Lightning Source directly, I could set a discount that was lower than the industry standard of 55 percent when dealing with the major distributors and booksellers, and the fee is only $12/year per title."

Daffron doesn't mind recommending LSI. She says, "Sign up with LSI as a publisher and set up your book with a 20 percent discount and no returns. And you don't have to deal with Amazon directly." This means that you no longer have to pay shipping to Amazon when they order a book. Daffron explains, "Lightning Source is able to manufacture books ordered by distribution partners so quickly that it takes the same amount of time as if they were "pulling" an already printed copy from a shelf in a warehouse somewhere."

Get Involved with Appropriate Websites

This is something that many authors don't think of doing, yet it can be so important to the success of your book. Become affiliated with websites related to your book's theme/genre. If your book relates to gardening, for example, become familiar with gardening websites. Find those that sell books at the site, that have recommended book pages and/or that have newsletters/blogs. Maybe you've written a romance novel; locate sites that focus on romance novels and study each of them to find out how they can afford you additional exposure for your book. Your method of gaining exposure through one site might be completely different than those you would pursue through other sites. You might volunteer to review books for a site, for example. How can this benefit you? You are listed at the site as a reviewer and the author of "such and such" book. You can list this credit (book reviewer for ABC website) in your byline and resume.

Maybe yours is a book on using intuition in the workplace. Seek out corporate sites. Offer to let them publish some of your useful articles at their site. Leave positive and useful comments at their blog site, write articles for their newsletter, etc. Some organizations and companies organize conferences and other events. By making yourself known to the leaders and directors, you may be able to get a speaking slot at some of them.

Likewise, get involved with public relations firms that organize events for companies and organizations. If your book is on a subject of wide interest or it is highly entertaining, you might be able to get speaking engagements at a variety of conferences and meetings. (See chapter eleven for more about public speaking.)

Sell Books through eBay

eBay is an auction site featuring an incredible array of items for sale. You can sell your books there for a price. They take a percentage of what you sell plus a fee for placing your book on eBay. Is it worth-while? I've found it so. It's kind of fun, too. Check out the various options for sellers at *www.ebay.com*.

Use Craigslist to Sell Books

Yes, you can even sell books on Craigslist. Just set a price, post your items, and collect paychecks.

www.craigslist.org.

Give Something in Order to Get Something

When we become authors, we begin to focus on selling, selling, selling. We are sometimes so motivated to sell our books that we miss great opportunities to promote them. One such opportunity involves donating copies of our books.

Donate Books

There are many ways to donate books and many outcomes. Donate books at active websites and suggest they run contests. I've donated copies of my books to sites that regularly run contests and give away books as prizes. How does this affect your bottom line? Your book is featured front and center at this website and, perhaps, in a newsletter for anywhere from a week to a month or more. That's a great exposure moment. Also, someone receives a copy of your book. If they like it, they will talk about it. You get more exposure, and we all know that exposure leads to sales.

Donate to your local library system; they are bound to order more copies if it is a library-quality book.

Donate to community and charity events. Many of them run silent or live auctions, and this is a good way to get your book noticed. Simply give one or two books for the auction or package a book attractively in a basket with related items. For a novel, this might be a candle, chocolate candy, a bookmark, and a pair of cozy slipper socks. I would package my Ojai history book with a couple of items made in Ojai—our Ojai olive oil, Ojai coffee, a coffee mug stamped with Ojai, and so forth. I might package the book you are holding with my hallmark book, *Publish Your Book: Proven Strategies and Resources for Enterprising Authors,* a pen advertising my publishing company (Matilija Press), a notepad, a button that says "I'm an author," and a booklight.

There's nothing like an auction to get your book noticed. If it is a silent auction, your book is displayed on a table throughout the entire event, and anywhere from fifty to a thousand people might see it and handle it. For a live auction, your book will be exhibited on a table for all to see and then it will be highlighted for a few minutes as the auctioneer talks about it in front of the crowd. Books donated for auctions, raffle drawings, and such also get press, and the titles and descriptions are generally published on handouts dispersed to everyone in attendance.

Donate your book for the raffle at the grand opening of a new car dealership. Give copies of your children's book to the newly formed youth foundation or the opening of a Boys & Girls Club. Provide copies for the annual fund-raiser/open house for a local private or public school. What are the benefits of donating books? Exposure leading to possible immediate or future sales and that good feeling that comes with giving. And your donation is a tax write-off.

Some authors connect their books to a charity—giving a percentage of the proceeds to a good cause. Does this practice foster sales? According to a PR Week/Barkley Cause Survey, nearly three-quarters of people surveyed said they purchase certain brands because they support a cause the consumer believes in.

If you have a book focusing on a particular health issue, pet rescue, illiteracy, or protecting pristine areas of the United States for example, you might want to partner with a related organization or agency by donating proceeds from your book to them. The pluses are, the "partner" may help to give your book wider visibility and their members/followers might be more inclined to purchase your book.

Renay Daniels is the author of *Ten Little Bulldogs,* an easy-to-read, count-to-ten book featuring color photographs of bulldog puppies. She actually created this book for Children's Miracle Network (CMN) in order to raise funds for children's hospitals. She says, "The Children's Miracle Network endorsed the book and now it has become an educational tool for them. Their logo is on the back of my book, and I continue to donate a percentage of the profits to them."

Daniels also donates copies to the Humane Society and to various bulldog rescue organizations. She says, "People feel good about purchasing a product that gives back, this is especially true for charities set up to help kids and animals." According to Daniels, "Book sales are key in all of this. The more books that sell, the more money the charity gets and so does the author."

She takes her book everywhere and shows it to everyone she meets. But her most successful event, yet, was her book launch party at an exclusive hotel and spa. "I sold over $800 worth of books that night."

What would she recommend to others who want to use their books to raise money for a cause? "Find out who's in charge. Get in front of them somehow. Show them your book and see if it is something they get excited about. Enthusiasm is the key. If they are enthusiastic about your book, they will want to help you take it to the next level." But she cautions, "The author must be proactive. Don't be afraid to brag about your book."

Provide Waiting Room Copies

When you receive a shipment of books from the printer or your publisher, open the boxes and check each book for flaws. Set aside those copies that are less than perfect and negotiate a full or partial refund from the printer or your pay-to-publish company. I've had books come straight from the printer with creases in the covers, uneven cuts on the flush edges of the pages, wrinkled pages, crooked pages, faint printing on a few consecutive pages, too much ink in places, pages missing, etc. Place slightly flawed books in waiting rooms throughout your city/county. I have left copies of my Ojai history book in several doctors', dentists', veterinarians', attorneys', and accountants' waiting rooms locally as well as in hospital lobbies.

Mark these "waiting-room copy." And just inside the front cover, post a list of local bookstores and specialty shops where the book can be purchased along with your ordering information.

This is a great way for your book to get exposure. But beware, many a waiting-room copy has disappeared, never to be recovered again. So you might want to check back occasionally and consider replacing missing books. Often, you'll find the book in the back office with the staff. In this case, encourage them to release it back to the waiting room. Offer employees a discount if they will purchase the book.

Offer Lunchroom Copies

Corporations, hospitals, schools, banks, government offices all have lunchrooms. For added exposure for your novel, in particular, leave copies in the lunchroom at key places along with plenty of order forms. Other books that might be appropriate as lunchroom copies are books related to history, business, finances, real estate, politics, and so forth.

Volunteer

I recommend volunteering your time especially on projects related to your book topic. If you have a book on growing herbs, volunteer to help out at a local community garden. If you've written a book on skateboards, volunteer to help build a local skateboard park or to offer classes in skateboarding or repairing skateboards for local youths. If you're the author of a book on hiking trails, donate your time guiding hikes.

I give historic tours aboard one of our city trolleys or a horse-drawn wagon during our annual Ojai Day celebration. Of course, I have the opportunity to talk about my books and always sell some.

My grandchildren and I were volunteers in a local adopt-a-grave program and this was an excellent arena in which to promote my Nordhoff Cemetery books (profiling early burials in our pioneer cemetery).

Many of my publishing and freelance writing workshops and presentations are offered on a volunteer basis.

Post Free Chapters

Provide a free chapter or two of your novel at your website in order to entice readers to purchase the entire book. For nonfiction, it is often enough to simply post your expansive table of contents. In fact, some authors post the chapter summaries from their book proposal at their websites.

Share Excerpts

Some magazines publish excerpts from nonfiction books on topics that fit with their themes. And many of them pay. This is another good way to get exposure for your book. *The Atlantic Monthly* uses book excerpts as do *Bibliophilos, Minnesota Conservation Volunteer, Earth Island Journal, Lake Superior Magazine, Rural Builder, Book Dealers World, School Transportation News, Teachers and Writers Magazine, Faith and Friends, Catholic Digest, Christian Home and School, Inventors Digest, Astronomy, GirlFriendz, Hope for Women, Strut* and many others.

How do you find out which magazines use excerpts? Study *Writer's Market*. This resource is available in most libraries and for around $30 at most bookstores.

Give Testimonials

Once your book is published, offer to endorse other books on your topic or in your genre. I've written testimonials that have appeared on the covers of books on California history, spiritually, cooking, and writing/publishing as well as a few novels. What does giving endorsements or testimonials do for your book? It provides additional exposure to your audience and helps to position you as an expert in your field.

Most of the time, I am approached to write the testimonial. But you can also offer to do one. It's a little tricky to locate authors of books in the works because they don't usually promote their books until they are published. If you stay abreast of what's going on in your field/genre, however, you'll begin to hear about pending books, read about them in blogs, and find out about them through diligent visits to appropriate websites.

You don't have to wait for a new book opportunity, however. We're in the digital age, after all, and books are being revised and reprinted quite often these days. So if you offer testimonials for books by experts in your field, your words could end up on the cover of their revision or a new book on the subject. At the very least, your testimonial will go on the author's book page on his or her website.

Simply read the book; create a smashingly complimentary and articulate testimonial; give your name, the title of your book, and your website address; and then send it to the author to do with as he wishes. You might even suggest that the he post your comments on his blog, in his next newsletter, etc. Most authors have testimonials pages at our websites.

Maybe you feel a bit awkward about writing a testimonial—you just don't know what to say. No problem. Simply find out what others are saying about the book you are "reviewing." Look at the book page or testimonials pages at the author's website. Read the customer reviews and comments at his page on Amazon. Do a Google search to locate reviews of this book elsewhere.

Speaking of Amazon.com, be sure to post your comments on these authors' Amazon book pages for even greater exposure.

Try to be clever, but not so clever that your words have little meaning. Be flattering. Be succinct. And be honest. Honestly, if you think the book stinks, don't bother to affiliate yourself with it.

Create Amazing Handouts

People love receiving something unexpected, and free. I try to always provide some sort of handout when I speak, conduct workshops, do book signings, showcase my book at book festivals, and even to enclose with book shipments. I suggest that you do too. Your handouts might involve a bookmark, magnets, postcards, or brochures with a photo of your book and ordering information; creative business cards; articles or short stories tucked into a colorful folder or otherwise attractively packaged; a resource list pertinent to the topic or genre; and so forth.

Network with the Right People

Networking is the coming together of people for the purpose of sharing information. When you tell a reader about your book, discuss bookselling with a bookstore owner, or ask a colleague about his/her publicist, you are networking. Networking is a natural way to promote books. But it takes concentrated effort and a measure of protocol. You must be willing to put yourself out there—to mingle, participate in small talk, and even schmooze. Networking is a two-way connection. And there are many methods of networking and potential opportunities.

Join Clubs and Organizations

Meet and network with people who are, most likely, interested in the topic of your book.

Why? Because belonging puts you in touch. Join groups related to your topic/genre because this is, presumably, where your audience is. Attend meetings regularly and keep informed about happenings within your area of interest.

For example, let's say that your book is a how-to for people who love, collect, and wear vintage clothing. You'll want to join groups that include members who share your passion for vintage clothing and accessories. You might find some groups made up of antique or flea market followers. And, surely, your book will also sell to some of these consumers.

I know the author of a mystery novel featuring a woman banker. She often attends meetings of various businesswomen's groups and sells quite a few copies of her book in this environment.

Participate in Online Forums and Discussion Groups

Everyone is online these days, and most of us gravitate toward sites, groups and forums of like-minded people. Locate forums and discussion groups related to your book topic by doing a Google search, whether it is bulldogs, feral cats, grilling, growing and cooking with herbs, raising an autistic child, living with arthritis, or comic book collecting. Use keywords, "discussion group" or "forum" and your topic—"arthritis," "comic books," grilling," etc.

There's a difference between the way a forum and a discussion group is presented. Generally, you visit the forum to read and post messages. Messages posted within a discussion group arrive in your e-mail box and you can respond via e-mail.

The beauty of discussion groups and forums is that they are interactive—you have the opportunity to meet and get to know members of your reading audience. Nobody likes a know-it-all, but you can certainly offer help and information based on your level of expertise when appropriate.

Most discussion groups and forums are free—you just need to sign up and adhere to the site rules. Rules might include no porn, be kind to each other, and no blatant promotion allowed. How do you let people know about your book if you're not allowed to promote it through the forum? There are ways. Make sure to include your e-mail address, website information, and book title in your profile (where appropriate). For discussion groups, create a succinct "signature" that is automatically attached to your outgoing e-mails. (Learn more about an e-mail signature in chapter seven.) Further, you might respond to a post by quoting something from your book, where appropriate. Say, for example, "You're right about this particular herb needing more sun than most. But according to expert, Nadia Phillips, when I interviewed her for my book, *Growing the Best Herbs in the West*, 'A good way to provide that sun is to plant the seeds in a pot and move it according to the placement of the sunlight each day.'"

(Read about networking through social media in chapter eight.)

Glean Ideas from Other Authors

I like to suggest that authors eavesdrop and drop in on other authors who are writing in their genre/topic. Visit their websites and see what you can find out about how many books they are selling and how they are selling their books. What methods are they using? Where are they speaking? Where are their articles appearing? Who is reviewing their books? What are they offering customers, etc.?

You can get some of this information by studying authors' websites. Do they list their calendar of speaking events? Read their blogs. Check out their "media" pages to find out where they've had their books reviewed, what other methods of promotion they've used, and how effective it was. They might have an article posted about an unusual promotional activity through which they sold numbers of copies of their book. This might give you some ideas for promoting your similar book.

You might also do a Google search for their book and see where it shows up—where has it been mentioned and reviewed? Where is it offered for sale? You could even sign up for Google Alerts using this author or the subject or title of the book. Each day you will receive information about where this book is being featured, spoken about, reviewed, etc. (Read more about Google Alerts in chapter fourteen.)

Make contact with authors of books like yours. Discuss promotional ideas. If you share your successes generously, the other author will probably give in return.

Be a Resourceful and Imaginative Promoter

In case you haven't noticed by now, book promotion takes a large measure of creativity. This chapter is designed to encourage authors to step even further outside their self-manufactured boxes and get creative. Let's hope that these few ideas spark many more of your own.

Market According to Season

Some seasons are better than others for promoting your particular book. Take advantage of this. I typically promote my luau book around Father's Day. My cat stories book, *Catscapades*, sells well as a Valentine's Day or Mother's Day gift.

Most authors strive to have their books published in time for Christmas sales, but this isn't the best time to promote all books. And, what many authors and publisher don't know is how many other opportunities there are for seasonal marketing.

Did you know that in January, for example, we have National Hugging Day, Thank Your Customer Week, and Financial Wellness Month? January second is Happy Mew Year for cats. A few special reasons to celebrate in July include Family Reunion Month and Make a Difference to Children Month. Have you ever heard of Responsible Pet Owner's Month, National Tooth Fairy Day, or Read in the Bathtub Day?

How can you use these rather obscure and unusual prompts to promote your book? Here are a few ideas:

.

- Submit articles to appropriate magazines pointing up the special day or week and promote your book in your bio. For example, around election time, pitch an article to a dog magazine showing which former and present celebrity dog or story dog would make the best president and why. Mention your book on celebrity dogs in your bio. In honor of Financial Wellness Month, promote your book on tips for playing the stock market for the average Jill and Joe. If your book features volunteering as a family value, choose some of the many seasonal prompts that relate to volunteering and use them to develop articles designed to promote your book.

- If you have a children's book or a book of poetry, arrange to do readings at local libraries during any of the many literary observances.

- Develop presentations around some of the more interesting and obscure seasonal prompts and offer to entertain at civic group or organization meetings throughout your community.

- Create an event around a prompt that reflects the focus of your book. If your book focuses on relationships, consider launching a relationship fair in honor of National Hugging Day. You should also be able to organize a beach, park, or lake clean-up day to promote your book on all things green; produce a project that promotes literacy with your book on book clubs for kids; a community coupon exchange designed to promote your book on how to buy for less and; perhaps, a health and fitness workshop during wellness week to promote your book on this topic.

- Use a prompt as an excuse to start a charity—collect books, shoes, or coats for children; arrange for discounted microchip implants for pets; organize a childcare resource center in your community.

- Schedule book signings in unique environments to honor various little-known prompts—at a wrecking yard or your own back-yard, on a mountaintop at sunset, at the mall, at a coffee house, or dog show. Provide something that people can't resist, a truly interesting or exciting experience (a ride on a zip line, a white-water raft, or horseback), an unusual dining experience or freebies, for example.

This ought to give you some idea of the fun you can have promoting your book by the season. Following are sites where you can become acquainted with the many seasonal prompts.

www.brownielocks.com
www.holidayinsights.com
www.gone-ta-pott.com

Create Promotional Displays

Offer promotional aids to the bookstores and specialty shops that carry your book. Have an attractive point-of-purchase display created to hold your books. The store might agree to hang a colorful poster or a mobile advertising your book.

Have you ever noticed what attracts you when you're shopping? What sort of display catches your eye? Often, it is a colorful, attractive display that stands apart from the rest. For the best opportunity for your book, consider it an impulse item. This means that customers probably do not come into this store purposely to purchase your book. Those who buy it do so because it is conveniently displayed and they happen to see it, and the topic or genre is something they or someone they know is interested in. Or maybe they have seen the display in this store several times and finally got the money together to buy it. One thing is for sure—if the book was not offered for sale in that store and if it was not prominently and attractively displayed, it would not be racking up sales.

Consider ordering advertising pens, small calendars, or bookmarks for the bookseller to give away to customers. People love to get freebies. You can also hand some of these items out at book festivals and other events as well as offer them to folks who order your book from your website.

Order displays and promotional items here:

www.qualitylogoproducts.com
www.empirepromos.com
www.gopromos.com

Enter Contests

Bring added attention to your book by earning it some notability. If your book wins an award, send press releases to newspapers and related magazines. Order stickers for the cover of your book that say, "Award-winning book," or "Won first place in the WD Best Book Contest." In your next printing, have the award notice printed on the cover.

Find contests listed in *Literary Market Place, Writers Market,* and *World's Biggest Book of Writing Contests.* Watch for contest listings in writers'/publishers' magazines and newsletters and posted at writing/publishing websites. Also check the following sites:

www.bookspot.com/awards
www.readersread.com/awards

Most contests have strict rules. Make sure that you are entering with the appropriate qualifications. Check the guidelines carefully. Is this contest open to published or unpublished books? What are the requirements for the publication date? Are there restrictions as to the mode of publication? Some contests prohibit self-published books, for example. Choose the category and/or genre carefully to avoid disqualification and to give your project the best chance possible. Make sure that you adhere to the deadline and send the correct entry fee. Some contest rules are complicated and confusing. If you have questions, e-mail or call the organizers.

Even if you win third place or honorable mention, you can represent your book as an award-winning book and yourself as an award-winning author. I suspect that some people I meet fudge on their award status. I do not recommend that you do this. If your book was among ten finalists, but ultimately came in at number six, you cannot ethically say that you were a first-place winner.

Design Contests

Bring attention to your book by creating a contest that relates to your book topic/genre. If you have a book of poetry, run a poetry contest. If you wrote a cookbook, establish a cooking or recipe competition.

Your publishing company could run a contest for the best title for your upcoming book.

Advertise your contest through flyers, classified ads in related magazines, news releases to newspapers and club/organization newsletters, and in your bio at the end of your magazine/e-zine articles.

Spend Some Money in All of the Right Places

While this book features no- and low-cost book promotion ideas, I include this chapter with good reason. There are projects and occasions that may require hiring people to help with promotion. If your book is conducive to major sales, then consider paying the appropriate individual or entity to help. This might include a novel that has been well received, a promising celebrity memoir, a true crime based on a well-known case, or a children's book that is getting a lot of attention.

Probably your book on ten ways to get rid of garden snails, how to shop for a purse, my life with an alcoholic, or raisin recipes would not benefit enough from a pricey promotional campaign to risk spending the money. Generally, if you are shopping for a publicist, for example, a good one will honestly evaluate the potential for your particular book.

Hire a Publicist

Hiring a good publicist is not cheap; but it can be highly effective, if even just to jump-start your sales. To find a publicist, look on the acknowledgements pages of books similar to yours. Often the publicist will be listed there. Also contact the Public Relations Society of America, *www.prsa.org,* or in Canada, *www.cprs.ca.*

The authors I've known who hired effective publicists had amazing success with their books. One author told me, "I was busier than I've ever been in my life, during those months when I was working with my publicist. I sold an awful lot of books."

A book publicist does not do the promotion, nor does he/she make the sale. A good publicist knows how to position you before your audience. She will negotiate to get you media interviews, speaking engagements, book signings, and other opportunities. A publicist can cost around $3,000/month, but if you will work with him or her, it can be exhausting, but well worth the expense.

Employ Sales Representatives

When I self-published my first book that could be marketed nationally rather than just locally, I came up with the idea of asking friends and e-mail pals in other cities to be my sales reps for their regions. The idea was that I would pay a commission on the books they sold to individuals and that they placed in bookstores.

I didn't follow through completely with this idea, but it may work for you. With so many people out of work, surely, you have friends who would like to earn a little money by showing your book around to their friends, arranging for it to be purchased by libraries and bookstores, walking press releases into newspaper offices, setting up gigs for you on local radio stations, getting it read in local book clubs, etc.

I would offer 30 percent of the cover price to your reps for individual sales and, since the bookstore gets 40 percent, give your rep 20 percent of your profit for bookstore sales. For a $19.95 book, that is $5.98 for books sold to individuals and $2.39 for each book sold through stores. If your rep sells twenty-five books to individuals and fifty books through bookstore and other retail stores, he/she will earn $269.00. This ought to motivate some of your out-of-work friends or maybe a college student who needs some extra cash.

Add to Your Line of Books

Produce spin-offs. A spin-off is a book on a topic related to your original book. If you're doing fairly well with one book, consider adding others.

When I came out with a book profiling the early burials at our local pioneer cemetery, many of the people who had purchased my Ojai history book were interested in this one. Customers, who bought any of my earlier books for authors, are often eager to purchase my newer books on publishing and book promotion.

Here are some of the ways you can benefit from publishing a line of books:

- You gain greater credibility as an expert in your field or as a writer in your genre.
- When you give presentations, you have more books to offer and you make more sales.
- If your original book is selling well through bookstores and specialty stores, these booksellers will most likely welcome your other books on that topic or in that genre.
- You can apply the same marketing techniques to all of the books in your line.

Instead of writing a full-blown book, you could offer customers additional or related material in the form of pamphlets, booklets, or e-books. If your book is on landscaping, for example, produce pamphlets featuring poolside landscaping tips, how to choose the right shade tree for your yard and your family, or planting and using the kitchen herb garden. Your travel book might attract more interest if you came out with pamphlets focusing on inexpensive travel tips, how to pack for any adventure, or tips for staying fit and healthy while traveling. I know someone who doesn't pack to travel. She buys clothes at thrift stores once she arrives at her destination and takes them back when she is ready to fly home. Wouldn't that be an interesting concept for a pamphlet?

You can sell e-books through Amazon.com and other outlets, but they must have an ISBN. Sell e-books through *www.ebookmall.com* or *www.diesel-ebooks.com*.

Sandra Jones Cropsey spins her books into plays. In fact, she has had the thrill of seeing two of her books performed as plays. Her children's book, *Tinker's Christmas,* aired as a radio drama in 2008 and her novel, *Who's There,* was performed on stage locally in 2010. She says of the process, "Taking a 221-page published work and condensing it to a 109-page working script is like stripping an automobile down to its body and then building it back with only the essentials." She says that the process of turning written works into a play is "much the same as starting a novel, only a lot more attention is given to action and motivation."

She talks about the experience of watching her characters come to life on stage: "Words that began as scribbles on a page developed a life of their own, and I reveled in the wonder of the creation."

Not every book is conducive to becoming a play. Cropsey suggests to those who dream of seeing their story performed, "Attend workshops, conferences, and seminars. Read plays—lots of them. Go to the theater and join a playwriting group, if available, or a writing group." She encourages budding playwrights to participate in critique sessions. She says, "Hearing the words read out loud, and preferably by others, will offer tremendous insight into what is working in your play in progress and what is not."

Create Other Items Related to Your Book

Gimmicks help to sell books. If you have a book of 101 ways to cook an egg, sell more copies by packaging it with a small frying pan, designer spatula, an eggcup, or special seasoning. Or simply offer these items for sale separately. People who buy the item might also buy the book and vice versa.

The author of a book featuring how to make Christmas tree ornaments might be inspired to create Christmas tree ornament kits.

For a novel, come up with something depicting an aspect of your story or simply package it with a book light, creative bookmark, or a box of chocolates, for example.

Children's book authors sometimes have the book's characters replicated in stuffed animals or puppets to package with the book or to sell separately.

Buy Ads to Entice Your Readers

Advertising can be costly, but sometimes necessary. It's wise to assess the situation before plunking down hundreds or thousands of dollars.

Will it pay you to drop $18,000 for a one-page ad in the *New York Times* Book Review section? Probably not unless you are a giant in the industry. It's likely that you will get more for your money with several smaller ads in an appropriate magazine spread over time than with one flashy ad.

Consider advertising in newsletters that relate to the subject of your book. It's inexpensive and can be worthwhile.

Many authors and publishers solicit ads for their websites. Look into affiliate marketing, for example. (Read more about affiliate marketing in chapter seven.)

www.affiliateseeking.com
www.affiliatetips.com
Directory of Affiliate Programs
www.100best-affiliate-programs.com

Christy Pinheiro markets her books and other materials designed for accounting, finance, and tax professionals entirely online. She says, "I have dedicated websites for my books, and I maintain them and update them frequently." While she ventures out into the wide world of online promotion opportunities, her ultimate goal is to bring customers back to her website (or to Amazon.com) to purchase her books and audiobooks.

According to Pinheiro, "Adwords (those ads on Google search results pages), solicited reviews (from accountant exam candidates), and forum postings are my most effective methods of marketing. I post regularly to professional message boards, and I can see from my web reports that about one-third of my web hits are from those posts. The remainder is almost all generated from Adwords."

She has some ideas for making her books and her website pay in a new way. She says, "I'm using the books to morph into another business—online CPE (Continuing Professional Education). She says, "I'm having a new website built. I already have the materials. All I have to do is generate the exams. It's a good way to make passive revenue from the material I already have."

Her advice for authors who are contemplating a website, "Don't use a crappy free website that just screams 'amateur.' A good website can be had for $15 per year through Microsoft Live. There's no excuse for not having an online presence."

Create Advertising Tools

We've talked about having brochures and promotional items such as postcards, magnets, pens, and bookmarks made. Purchase these in large quantities and feel free to leave a few everywhere you go—the library, city hall, grocery store, flea market, restroom at local restaurants, etc.

Have a button made that says "Ask me about my book." Display a photo of your book on a tee shirt and wear it to book festivals, book signings, or to Disneyland, for example.

Here are three places that make promotional items.
www.qualitylogoproducts.com
www.empirepromos.com
www.gopromos.com

Let Your Book Cover Sell Books

Create posters from your book cover and use them to attract attention for your book at book festivals, while speaking or doing book signings, for example. But make sure it is an attractive cover. In fact, let me stress the importance of having your cover professionally designed.

I have participated in many book festivals and I can tell you that the books that get the most attention from visitors are those that are attractive, sharp, and clear. I remember one festival in particular where the author of one book sat while watching visitor after visitor bypass her all day long. I don't think that anyone stopped to even take a second look at her book let alone pick it up and study it more closely. This book was dull; the design was a muddy dirty gold shade with no real definition. You could barely read the lettering, so you didn't even know what the book was about. That day, the book that was picked up most was an attractive book on grammar! I'm convinced that it was the cover that sold so many copies of the grammar book that day. People liked the look of it, loved the clever title, and most of them picked it up to check it out further. While holding it, many of them envisioned either using it or giving it to someone who could use it. And they bought it.

Have posters of your book cover made at a local business center.

Go the Extra Mile for Your Customers

Even if you have only one book to sell, treat every customer as if you expect or desire their return business. Make every customer feel valued. If you do, they are more apt to come back and purchase additional copies of your books. They'll surely talk about you and your book to their friends. If you decide to produce another book, a spin-off item, or develop a workshop, you'll want satisfied customers to fall back on.

Sometimes good customer service is simple—your transactions are impeccably and easily orchestrated. Other times, you are required to go to many lengths in order to make a sale. All authors and publishers have their horror stories. I share one of mine below.

Encourage Repeat Customers by Doing Good Business

What comprises good business practices? How do you make a good impression?

- Communicate clearly with your customers.
- Provide what you promise in your advertising.
- Make all transactions as smooth and easy as possible.
- Give something more than your customer expects.
- Pack books so they arrive undamaged.
- Ship in a timely manner.
- Handle any problems promptly, cheerfully, and satisfactorily.

I like the idea of giving something more than customers expect. I know one author who wraps her poetry book in pretty tissue paper and ties it with a piece of ribbon before sliding it into the padded mailer to ship. I enclose a gift magnet with the image of the book cover with shipments of my cat stories books. It's fairly easy to please a satisfied customer. The real challenge comes when something goes wrong with the order.

One author I know inadvertently shipped out a box of books that included a couple of flawed books. When the customer explained the problem, my friend replaced the books at no charge and even returned the customer's original payment for those two books in order to maintain good customer relations.

A few years ago, a customer called me to say that the Ojai history book I sold him had a signature of pages missing. To keep things simple and to take care of the problem quickly, I did not ask him to return the damaged book. I immediately shipped him a new book. And to further repair customer relations, I enclosed a copy of my *Nordhoff Cemetery* book as a bonus. This man will not hesitate doing business with my company again, and he may even tell others about Matilija Press and Patricia Fry.

Sometimes an author/publisher is asked to go beyond what should be reasonably expected, and sometimes the author loses. As an example, a few years ago, a gentleman from Australia ordered one of my books through my website. He contacted me almost immediately after making the transaction to say that his card was charged several times, but he only wanted one copy of the book. I checked my merchant account system, and sure enough, his card had been charged eleven times. He admitted to having clicked "buy" maybe twice, but not eleven times.

This was my first experience with this sort of problem and it was a slow go. When I completed the tedious process of hand-crediting his card, I contacted the customer and he claimed that I was still charging him for two copies of the book.

What? I double-checked carefully and discovered that I had accidentally inserted the wrong credit card number in one instance while attempting to issue him the appropriate credit. Turns out it was a valid credit card number and it greedily accepted the credit.

I didn't know what to do, so I called the tech people for my merchant account system and they advised me to simply charge that same card in order to retrieve my money. I issued my customer one more credit in the amount of the book and I attempted to charge the card that I had erroneously credited. Guess what? This card was red-flagged. It was under some sort of investigation and could not be charged. I never did get that money back. Consequently, for all of my trouble and time (because of a situation caused by the customer), I ended up with zilch. Regardless, I sent him the book he ordered.

Not every transaction is flawless. That's for sure. But you will make more friends and attract more customers (including repeat customers) if you do your best to keep things simple and if you will give the customer the benefit of the doubt.

Learn How to Sell Books Face-to-Face

I've spent a lot of time selling books at book festivals and other venues, and I've learned a lot from my own experiences and mistakes. I've also observed many other authors at work selling their books. Here are a few things that I've picked up:

Don't oversell your books. No kidding, I've watched as authors practically had the potential customer reaching in his or her pocket for money to pay for the book, when all of a sudden the deal goes sour. The customer, who seemed so enthralled with the book at first, suddenly becomes disinterested. He hems and haws a bit and then walks away. What happened? In many cases, the author oversold the book. Once the customer was ready to make the purchase, the author should have stopped trying to make the sale. The sale was made. It was a done deal. But he couldn't resist spewing more facts and even putting a bit of a hard-sell on the potential buyer.

Folks, overselling is one way to lose the sale. Once the customer has agreed to take the book, stop talking about it. Change the subject. Avoid any additions to your sales pitch unless the customer seems to be changing his mind or unless he asks additional questions.

Another thing that many authors neglect to do is ask for the sale. Yes, ask for it. Give your spiel; let the potential customer hold the book and thumb through it. Engage him in conversation about his herb garden, his pet, his writing project, his flying experiences, (depending on the topic of your book), and before he can put the book down and walk away, ask for the sale. Say, for example, "Will you be paying by credit card or cash today? I also take checks," "How many copies do you want?" "Purchase the book today and I'll give you a 20 percent discount."

I didn't believe the wisdom in this suggestion at first. But, when I began to practice asking for the sale, I was surprised to learn that it is a valuable and often successful technique.

Make it Easy for Customers to Buy Your Books

Most people have a favorite way of purchasing things—some write checks while other typically use their credit cards. There are people who love the convenience of shopping by computer, but who much prefer using PayPal to sending their credit card information through unfamiliar sites. There are those who will only buy with cash in person and many people in between with preferences for ordering things either by phone, fax, or mail.

Make it easy for all of these customers to buy your book by providing every available method of purchasing. A message machine that takes orders is ideal for a busy office and a convenience for customers. Consider an e-commerce website. But first, you need to set up a merchant account (an account through which you can accept credit cards).

Start by checking with your own bank. Watch for special offers for merchant accounts through organizations such as IPBA or SPAN. Or hook up with a company or organization that will take orders for you through their merchant account system for a fee.

Some authors/publishers worry about accepting checks. While there is always some risk of loss, when it comes to books, it seems minimal. In thirty years of bookselling, I've never been given a bad check. I've had customers skip out on paying me altogether once or twice, but I've never been given a bad check. I like to think that book buyers/readers have more integrity than some others. (Read more about setting up a merchant account in chapter seven.)

Give Customers More Than They Expect

We all enjoy receiving more than we expect. How can you surprise, delight, or otherwise please your customers? We've mentioned a few tools to use in book promotion—bookmarks, magnets, pens, etc. Pack one of these items with book shipments. Use one of your spin-off products as a tuck-in gift for customers, especially those who purchase more than one of your books.

Use your imagination to come up with ideas that will compliment your book. Visit sites that create advertising materials for ideas, a mouse pad, tote bag, fortune cookies, or travel kit, for example. Create a calendar with a photo of your book or photos from inside the book, give packages of flower or veggie seeds, or design a work-book to accompany your book orders during special sales campaigns, when the customer orders more than one book or for repeat custom-ers. Here are a few websites with promotional materials:

www.superiorpromos.com
www.vistaprint.com
www.choicepromotionalproducts.com

Develop a Professional Telephone Persona

Most bookstore owners and distributors send purchase orders by e-mail or fax. Others will call with orders. Individual customers will sometimes call, as well. Be prepared.

When you work out of a home office, you're not always in profes-sional mode. Rather than using the family telephone for orders, consider having a separate line installed for business calls. This is especially important if you are going to do a lot of radio and TV shows. Then you will want to install an 800 number with a message machine for taking orders when you are not in the office.

Record Your Book on Tape for the Blind and the Busy

Sell more copies of your book by making it available to nonreaders—those who enjoy books on tape. Who listens to books on tape? Artists who are working on projects, young mothers who are busy with small children, people who drive long distances, and those who are losing or who have lost their sight. Here are a few sites where you can learn about getting your book on tape:

www.spokenbookspublishing.com
www.audiocdlearn.com
http://teach.learnoutloud.com

Tap into the Library Market

There are approximately 122,000 libraries in the United States. This includes public libraries as well as university, private and public school, academic, medical, law, and other specialty libraries. If you have a book that is suitable for library use (it has a sturdy binding and appropriate subject matter), you'll want to approach libraries. They generally pay full price for books when they purchase directly from the publisher. (But librarians do like to get a discount.)

Many libraries today purchase books through various wholesalers such as Baker and Taylor and Quality Books. (See contact info at the end of this chapter.) The American Library Association (ALA) estimates that libraries purchase as many as three-quarters of their books through distributors and wholesalers. So there is still a chance that you can do business with libraries. Following are some ideas for landing those purchase orders from libraries.

Donate Books to Libraries

Consider donating your book to pertinent libraries—your own college library, your hometown library, the library in the city where your story takes place, etc. I always donate one or more copies of my newly published books to our local library. This is a generous way to introduce your book to the library system and the community. I've also sent copies to large library systems throughout the United States along with my ordering information. In most cases, if the book is of library quality, they will order additional copies.

Another good reason for donating books to libraries is to get it in the system where numbers of readers are seeing it. Some patrons might actually go out and buy copies. If the book is requested often, the librarian may be inclined to order more copies.

Do Readings at Libraries

Visit libraries locally and while traveling and offer to give readings. This is particularly effective for fiction, poetry, and children's books. Sometimes the librarian will allow you to sell books if you donate a percentage of the proceeds to the library.

Before getting too excited about doing readings, make sure that you have excellent reading skills. Join a storytelling group or take a drama class to learn how to use vocal variety, how to use emphasis and pauses effectively, and for tips for using props, puppets, and so forth. These things will contribute to a much more entertaining reading.

Solicit Orders from Libraries Nationwide

If your book is sturdy enough and otherwise qualifies for inclusion in libraries, you might do very well by tapping into the library market.

Make your book suited to library use. Have it perfect or hardbound rather than spiral bound or saddle-stitched, for example. Create an index for your nonfiction book—librarians and researchers love indexes. Librarians try to maintain a good stock of best-selling books.

According to an article in the *Library Journal*, 2009, library purchases account for over 10 percent of industry book sales. And libraries represent about 40 percent of the children's book market.

While libraries generally pay full price, they also appreciate a discount. So take this into consideration.

Librarians purchase books based on patron recommendations, so the promotion that you are doing outside of the library could also help your library sales. Exhibiting your books at library tradeshows is another way to get your book noticed. Library acquisitions directors also read prepublication and postpublication book reviews. I've even heard that librarians read reviews on some of the online book review sites. But like booksellers, they often make purchases through their distributors. (See a few of them listed below.)

To find out if your book is in the library system and which libraries have it, check out this site: *www.worldcat.org.*

Here are some library directories:
http://travelinlibrarian.info/libdir
www.publiclibraries.com
www.americanlibrarydirectory.com

Library Wholesalers

Baker and Taylor, Inc.
www.btol.com btinfo@btol.com
1-800-775-1800
Ingram Book Company
www.ingrambook.com
One Ingram Blvd.
La Vergne, TN 37068
Quality Books
www.quality-books.com

Some authors are hesitant to approach libraries for a variety of reasons. Bobbi Florio Graham dispels most of them. She says, "Librarians don't care who published the book. They do care about whether your promotional material looks completely professional. This means a cover that is original—doesn't use an obvious stock photograph or wacky fonts (unless it's a humor book) and the back cover copy has a compelling description, a full bar code with ISBN, personal testimonial, and a brief bio."

She recommends that you should approach a library in person, if you can. "Start with your local library and those within driving distance. Also take copies of your book when you travel and be prepared to leave a copy along with a promo package with every librarian you visit."

Graham reminds us, "Libraries pay full price. And there are no returns. People who borrow books often decide to buy their own copies." For this reason, she urges authors to include full ordering info inside their books. She shares this anecdote, "I've had a woman on the other side of Canada order my writing book six times. She bought her copy after borrowing it from the library several times and then wanted copies to give friends."

Promote Author Recognition Week

Get noticed in your community by recognizing other local authors. Ask the head librarian to sponsor local author month. Find authors in your community through writers' and publishers' groups, art centers, independent booksellers, and word of mouth. An article in the newspaper might also bring some previously unknown authors forward.

During the designated month, display the authors' publications at the library and ask each of them to spend an hour or an afternoon signing their books. To make this project even more attractive and more newsworthy, ask each author to donate a percentage of the proceeds from the sale of his books to the library. As the grand finale, maybe the library or a local bookstore will host an author reception.

Enhance Your Marketing Skills

Most authors approach book promotion with more hope than skills—more dreams than savvy. Universally, marketing is not the author's strong suit. That's why I compiled these 250-plus low- and no-cost promotional ideas. The following ten tips should greatly enhance your ability to apply numbers of them to your current and future book projects.

Join Trade/Genre Organizations

So now you are an expert in your field or genre. The last thing you want to do is shut out other experts or those from whom you can learn.

Join clubs and organizations related to the genre or subject/theme of your book. You'll learn new stuff, gain new perspectives, meet people you can interview or quote, obtain leads for speaking engagements, and more. Plus, this affiliation will add to your credibility in this field or genre.

Study Trends in Your Field or Genre

It is important that you know what's going on within your field or genre so that when you are interviewed about your book, or you're fielding questions while speaking, your responses are up to date, and reliable.

Once you've produced a book on a certain topic, you become known as an expert. Don't disappoint your readers and other followers. Keep abreast of new concepts in your area of expertise. You can't expect to write a book that is the "last word" on pets, publishing, quilting, cooking, parenting, health and fitness, or even raising goats. In this fast-paced world, within every topic/genre there are changes, new developments, innovative products, and original concepts.

Perhaps your book covers artwork in public buildings within your city or state. What could change about this topic? Art is stolen or damaged in natural disasters or it is replaced. New facts sometimes come to light on various pieces of art. It's important for you to keep up on these occurrences and facts and share them with your audience. In fact, that's the beauty of a blog or a newsletter.

I speak and write about publishing. And we all know how dramatically the publishing industry has changed within the last decade and, by the way, continues to change. There is something new to report about the industry, the key players, the playing field, individual companies and authors, and so forth, practically daily. And it is important that I keep up on what is transpiring. I urge you to do the same within your field or genre.

Continue Reading about Book Promotion

Never stop studying the complex subject of book promotion. Subscribe to Fran Silverman's *Book Promotion Newsletter*: *www.bookpromotionnewsletter.com*. I also recommend *Publishing Basics Newsletter*, *www.publishingbasics.com*, and the *SPAWN Market Update* (for SPAWN members only). Join here: *www.spawn.org*. IBPA and SPAN also have informative newsletters for members. Keep this book close at hand.

Join Publishing Organizations and Clubs

To learn more about what's going on in the publishing industry, join trade, professional, and networking organizations such as IBPA (Independent Book Publishers Association), *www.ibpa.org*; SPAN (Small Publishers, Association of North America), *www.spannet.org*; and SPAWN (Small Publishers, Artists and Writers Network), *www.spawn.org*.

There are also many regional publishing organizations and writers' groups. The folks at IBPA have affiliated with many regional organizations. Check with them to find one in your area. I occasionally list regional organizations in the *SPAWN Market Update* (posted monthly in the member area of the SPAWN website). So check with me—I might be able to help you find one. Also do a Google search to find a writers' group or publishing organization near you.

As a hopeful author and especially as a published author, you should be participating in organizations for authors, and publishers. Here is where you'll learn the business. You'll be privy to trends, you'll be exposed to book promotion ideas and resources and you'll probably be able to network with other authors.

While there are regional publishing organizations that meet face-to-face, the major publishing organizations are online.

www.spawn.org

www.ibpa-online.org

www.spannet.org

Do a Google search using keywords "publishing organization" or "author group" + your city, county or state. For example, "Author group Nashville" or "publishing organization Los Angeles."

Attend Writing/Publishing Conferences

There are writing and publishing conferences held all throughout the year in most major cities. But the premise of these conferences has changed over the years. The sessions at writers' conferences used to focus on character development, memoir writing, how to sell your magazine articles, and so forth. Now most of them also include workshops and other presentations for authors and independent publishers. You'll find sessions focusing on how to work with an agent, self-publishing tips, how to choose the right publishing option, cover design tips, and of course, book promotion.

At the time I was organizing this book, I found fifty conferences at one of these sites and seventy-six at the other. And most areas of the United States were represented—Kentucky, California, New Mexico, New Hampshire, Wyoming, New York, South Carolina, Texas, Hawaii, Nebraska, Washington State, and more. There are several conferences held outside of the United States as well, France, Amsterdam, London and Ghana, for example.

http://writing.shawguides.com

http://writersconf.org

Do a Google search to locate writers' conferences near you.

Before signing up for the first conference you find, study the offerings at various conferences. Find out who will be presenting workshops and on what topic. If you're not familiar with the speakers, visit their websites. Read their blogs. Take a look at their books and other writings. It may be that the conference in Baltimore is more suited to your needs than the one being held in your state.

Lastly, attend the conference with an open mind and realistic expectations.

Promote, Promote, Promote

You may have discovered already that your book will sell only for as long as you are willing to promote it. Slow down or stop promoting altogether and your book will stop selling.

A successful book depends on many things. First, it must be a book with a reasonable (not frivolous) purpose, it must be designed to attract a sizable segment of society, and it must be promoted to that audience. Successful long-term book sales depend on the author's long-term commitment to promoting it. So, before you decide to produce a book, especially if you hope for substantial sales, factor in time, energy, and creative ideas for promoting your book.

Create a Marketing Plan

The idea of creating a marketing plan can be as intimidating as being faced with writing a book proposal. But it can be as valuable. In fact, if you've written a full-blown book proposal, you have the beginnings of a marketing plan. Through writing your book proposal, you've become aware of your specific qualifications—skills, talents, connections—related to the task of marketing. You understand who your audience is and where they are. And, presumably, you know what it's going to take in order to reach them. This is the beginning of your marketing plan.

Let's say that you've decided to start promoting your book on eldercare by speaking before members of senior organizations, hospital and hospice workers, church groups, and at senior facilities. You also want to get some articles published in magazines pertinent to your topic. And you plan to build a website.

Log these tasks and start listing specific directors, program chairpersons, and editors that you will contact. Keep adding to these lists.

Don't stop there. While you continue this research, also consider the promotion you will do in the future. Maybe you know about a senior health and wellness event that is held annually in a nearby community. Make arrangements to participate. Collect information about these programs throughout your state and beyond. After attending the first one, you may decide if it is worth your time and money to travel to others.

Log other ideas you want to pursue—a press release blast to regional newspapers, teaching classes for local nurses and eldercare workers, developing a newsletter, etc.

Prioritize your ideas and do your best to create a schedule so you'll be more apt to stick to it.

Creating a marketing plan isn't difficult. But it does take something that many of us have trouble utilizing accurately—time, energy, and a sense of follow-through.

Design a Hotfile

Life has a way of racing past us while we're busy trying to keep up. And if you are promoting a book along with everything else that you do, it can become overwhelming. Think about it, how many good promotional ideas have escaped your grasp and been tossed aside simply because you are too busy or too preoccupied? That's why I suggest that you grab each promotional idea you stumble across, without judging it, and file it in your hotfile. When things calm down, your speaking circuit has slowed down, you've sent out your quota of press releases for the month, you've made several cold calls, open up the hotfile and see what's in there.

Here's what I hope you'll find waiting for you in there: leads for potential speaking engagements, information about a conference or trade show in your expertise, a new website devoted to the theme of your book, a list of magazines and newsletters related to your topic, the name of the new editor for a magazine you regularly submit articles to, and so forth.

Don't let another good (or even questionable) promotional idea escape you. File them in a red hotfile and always take the time at some point to acknowledge, evaluate, and in some cases, pursue the idea.

Track Your Sales

When mail order and catalog sales were the norm—before the advent of the Internet—authors/publishers had ways of tracking sales. We'd add different code numbers or letters to our addresses for each promotional outlet so we'd know where the sales were coming from. In other words, I might use "Dept. 130" in my address for one catalog I'm advertising in, "Dept. 110" in another, "Dept. 100" for promo material going out to my mailing list, and "Dept. 120" for the mailing lists I purchase. This is how we learned which promotional avenues were bringing in the most sales.

Today, we generally know where our orders are coming from, but we may wonder how the customer discovered us. You might want to add this question to your online order forms at your site and other places where you have your book for sale: "How did you hear about us?"

Surely you are logging each sale, so you know how many books you sold at the local flea market, the book festival in Atlanta, the trade show in Los Angeles, and to each of the various groups you visited throughout the year. Certainly, you log books sold at individual online and downtown retail stores. Periodically, tally sales and you'll discover where your books sell best. You'll want to continue pursuing these venues and outlets while kicking promotion in other areas up a notch or two.

Be Thankful

Don't get so caught up in the excitement of selling books and the challenges of creating a good marketing program that you forget to thank those who have helped you along the way. Send thank-you notes to book reviewers, booksellers who are moving quantities of your book, journalists who have written about you and your book, radio hosts who have talked about your project, organization leaders who have given you the opportunity to speak about your book, and people who have given you good promotional ideas.

There's nothing really hard about selling books, it's finding the customers that takes thought, time, and effort.

Use the foregoing list to develop a personal marketing plan. Set aside a sizable chunk of time each week to spend promoting your book. Express your assertiveness and persistence and you will surely be either mildly or wildly successful in your endeavors to sell books.

Good luck and good marketing.

CONTRIBUTORS

Cliff Ball has a BA in English and works as a freelance copy editor. He is the author of three novels, *The Usurper* (CreateSpace), *Don't Mess With Earth* (Virtualbookworm), and *Out of Time* (iUniverse). *http://cliffball.webs.com*

Cherie Brant is the author of books on historic Ventura County, California including *Keys to the County: Touring Historic Ventura County, Legends of Ventura County, Historic Railroads of Ventura County* and *Impossible Views: Birds-Eye Views of Ventura* (Del Sol Publications). She is a regular contributor to *Central Coast Farm and Ranch Magazine. www.venturamuseum.org*

Loree Griffin Burns, Ph.D., is the author of two books, *Tracking Trash: Flotsam, Jetsam, and the Science of Ocean Movement* and *The Hive Detectives: Chronicle of a Honey Bee Catastrophe* (Houghton Mifflin), and she is working on her third. *www.loreeburns.com*. Blog: *http://lgburns.livejournal.com.*

Marian Clayton recently published *Murder with a Twist*, a true crime story featuring a member of her family (MC Enterprises).

Sandra Jones Cropsey is the author of *Who's There* (Outskirts Press), a finalist in the 2008 Georgia Author of the Year Awards and *ForeWord Magazine's* Book of the Year Awards. *Who's There* was produced by the Main Street Players in 2010. Her children's book, *Tinker's Christmas* (Wright Books), was aired as a radio drama in 2008. *www.sandracropsey.com*

Susan Daffron is the president of Logical Expressions Inc., which is a book publishing and software company based in Sandpoint, Idaho. She is the author of eleven books and also the president of the Small Publishers, Artists and Writers Network (SPAWN). *www.logicalexpressions.com*

Renay Daniels is the author of *Ten Little Bulldogs* (Padden Publishing). She donates the proceeds from this children's book to the Children's Miracle Network. *www.tenlittlebulldogs.com.*

Meagan Francis is the author of four books, including *The Happiest Mom: 10 Secrets To Enjoying Motherhood* (Weldon Owen) and *One Year to an Organized Life with Baby* (Da Capo). She can be found online at *www.thehappiestmom.com.*

Bobbi Florio Graham is an award-winning author, teacher, and communications consultant who lives in Canada. The author of three books, *Five Fast Steps to Better Writing, Five Fast Steps to Low-Cost Publishing* and *MEWSINGS/MUSINGS* (Simon Teakettle Ink), she has contributed to thirty-five anthologies in Canada, the United States, Norway, and Sweden. *www.SimonTeakettle.com.*

Dena Harris is the author of *Lessons in Stalking: Adjusting to Life with Cats* (Spotlight Publishing) and *Who Moved My Mouse? A Self-Help Book for Cats (Who Don't Need Any Help),*(Ten Speed Press) *www.selfhelpforcats.com.*

Gerri Helms, CAM, CEG, CSC, is the author of *Trust God and Buy Broccoli, a Spiritual Approach to Weight Loss* (Love Your Life Publishing) and an e-book, *Seasons of Spirituality*. She is also a contributing author to *The Art of Grandparenting* (Nightengale Press). *www.lifecoachgerri.com*

Carolyn Howard-Johnson is the award-winning author of the How to do It Frugally series of books for writers, including *The Frugal Editor, The Frugal Book Promoter,* and *The Great First Impression Book Proposal. www.HowToDoItFrugally.com*

Karon Korp is the author of *Remembering Our Spiritual Journey Home: The 12 Keys for Awakening the Memory of Who You Are and Why You Are Here* (Magic Mountain Press). When not on the road speaking to groups about finding their true passion and purpose in life, she works as a community organizer and fund-raiser for non-profit and civic organizations. She is working on her next book about 2012 and the Mayan Calendar.

Marcia Meier is an award-winning journalist, writing coach, and the former director of the Santa Barbara Writers Conference. She is also the author of *Navigating the Rough Waters of Today's Publishing World, Critical Advice for Writers from Industry Insiders* (Quill Driver Books). *www.navigatingpublishing.com, www.marciameier.com.*

Marilyn Meredith is the author of the Deputy Tempe Crabtree mysteries (Mundania Press) and Rocky Bluff P.D. crime novels, which she writes under F.M. Meredith, (Oak Tree Press). Her latest book is *Lingering Spirit. http://fictionforyou.com.* Blog: *http://marilynmeredith.blogspot.com.*

Christy Pineiro, EA, ABA, is an enrolled agent, accredited business accountant, and writer. She is the owner of PassKey Publications, a publishing company that focuses on technical material for accounting and tax professionals. *www.passkeypublications.com*

Debbie Puente is a professional writer and cookbook author. Visit *www.examiner.com* to read her musings on food and friendship. You can find Debbie's column by typing in her full name in the search bar. Also, you can find Debbie on twitter: DebFriendship.

Penny C. Sansevieri, CEO and founder of Author Marketing Experts, Inc., is a best-selling author of five books, including *Red Hot Internet Publicity* which has been called the "leading guide to everything Internet." She is also an internationally recognized book marketing and media relations expert. *www.amarketingexpert.com*

Tweed Scott is a professional speaker and author and the author of *Texas in Her Own Words* (Redbud Publishing Company). *www.tweedscott.com.*

Rosie Sorenson is the award-winning author of *They Had Me at Meow: Tails of Love from the Homeless Cats of Buster Hollow* (Buster Hollow Productions) *www.theyhadmeatmeow.com.*

Carol White, coauthor of the award-winning book, *Live Your Road Trip Dream,* is also a publisher, speaker, article-writer, and book marketing coach. Her expertise is in helping other authors learn how to market their books. *www.carolwhitemarketing.com*

Diana Zimmerman is the author of *Kandide and the Secret of the Mists* (Scholastic Books). *www.kandide.com*

APPENDIX

Sample Marketing Plan 1
By Susan Daffron

Vegan Book Action Plan

Marketing Activity
Market, promote, and sell Vegan Success book

Intended Results of Marketing Activity
To have the book be recognized as a good source of recipes for the vegetarian community.

Many vegetarians know about and have bought the book.

Veggie press has positively reviewed and provided ad vehicle for the book.

Your Target Market—Who you will approach?
Vegetarian cooks looking for new ideas.

Non-vegetarians who want to learn more about vegetarian cooking.

New vegetarians who are mystified by vegetarian ingredients.

Organic growers/gardeners who are interested in vegetarian recipes because they have produce they need to use.

Sustainable agriculture, food co-op, buy local groups to stimulate people to buy produce.

Alternative health practitioners (naturopathic, etc.) who recommend low-fat/low cholesterol diets.

Basic Game Plan—Strategy and tactics

Promotion . . .

- Set aside some books to give away—send out for reviews in *Vegetarian Times, Veggie Life*
- Add recipes into Many Veggie Web site and ads on all LEI sites for cookbook
- Create autoresponder series (topic as yet unknown)
- Contact other vegetarian-related sites about ads and linking
- Write articles for free article sites on being vegan; recipes
- Press releases to PR Web and local media (investigate CdA culinary magazine?)
- Look into animal rights sites/newsletters
- Send copy to famous veggies, e.g. Molly Katzen, Robin Robertson, Lindsay Wagner

Marketing/Sales . . .

- Classified ads in certain magazines—*Mother Earth News*
- Consign at Winter Ridge and Truby's (and other health food stores)

Other . . .

- Try and find testimonials for cover of second edition (maybe from people who get it for free?)
- Look into Vegetarian associations, e.g. Vegetarian Resource Group—look in libraries
- Are there opportunities for partnership with food companies that benefit from vegan recipes, like Tofutti. (We're promoting recipes that use their product.)
- Investigate possible trade shows related to vegetarian living.

Message/Attention—Audio Logo—Ultimate Outcome

When you're vegan, figuring out what's for dinner can be a challenge. *Vegan Success* gives you scrumptious, healthy vegan recipes for busy people. (Great tasting fast food for people who don't eat fast food!)

Marketing Materials—What written or other materials will be needed?

- Autoresponder course
- Press release
- Web site copy and graphics
- Letters to people receiving free copies/reviews

Heart of Activity—Central part of your marketing plan

The heart of the marketing approach is the book itself. The book will be professionally printed and comparable in appearance to other commercially available recipe books.

Offer and Call to Action—How and when will you ask for action?

The ability to buy the book will be prominently displayed on promotional pages. The book itself will also have order forms in the back and a note that says it can be purchased in bulk in the front.

Follow-Up—How and when will you follow up?

We will follow up with people who receive free/review copies.

Action Steps and Timeline

Action Step	Due Date	Comp Date
Complete manuscript!! (Change the template to new design, input changes also include x-ref stuff, redo cover art in InDesign, create PDF files for Lightning Source initial review copies.)		

Get bar code		
Get ABI listing forms from RR Bowker		
Get LCCN number		
Write press release		
Research vegetarian sites for linking		
Update Many Veggie Recipes site		
Write sales page for book		
Write autoresponder course		

While book at printer . . .

Action Step	Due Date	Comp Date
Research more media people to send book to		
Create acknowledgement card for reviewers		
Create prepublication offer for personal mailing lists		
Get copyright forms from Copyright office		
Look into listing in various directories (Dust Books)		
Research Amazon.com and B&N sales		
Research book club sales/rights (look in LMP)		

After initial books are back from printer . . .

Action Step	Due Date	Comp Date
Mail out review copies		
Update LEI sites		

Send out press releases		
Write articles for free article sites		
Talk to health food stores about consignments		
Contact health food companies		
Give copies to clients/BNI members		
Mail to lists in *Complete Guide to Self-Publishing*		

Sample Marketing Plan 2

Strategic Positioning of the Book—*The Responsible Business*—
by Carol Sanford

Three aspects of this proposed strategy are: *Value proposition* or what the book provides that is unique and timely in its value; a *Brand* which denotes what space the book and author can "own" with market credibility; and the *product offering* which describes both what the book buyer gets that is not available in other offerings, and what adds something new to a field or domain.

These ideas are based on a competitive review of other contemporary books in the same domains or categories, using the above criteria. A detailed analysis of nine related books follows the strategy description below.

1. **Value Proposition: No Trade-offs**—corporate responsibility, sustainability as add-ons, important but separate from the real work of managing and operating a business has left companies and their managers in the position of continually making trade-off between competing priorities. This book shows companies how they can make CR an enterprise-wide and stakeholder-inclusive process by embedding conscious responsibility into the day to day work design and strategy development. Instead of feeling like they are

constantly making trade-offs, managers can see how they can utilize a systemic understanding to create greater synergy and leveraged effect.

2. **Brand for the Book: Wholeness for the Whole Business—Systemic Practice of a Responsible Corporate Enterprise.** The future of CSR is moving, and is likely to look a lot more like product innovation has been for a few really successful companies over the years. The companies that are serious about responsibility for the whole of their company and the wholeness of their business are looking for something new and meaningful, not more examples of best practices in their different functions and departments. They already know that CR pays back in business ways, that it is critical to image and brand and that there are now exemplar practices on every corner of the globe from thousands of companies. It is true that CR will help reputation and public relations, but only if it is a better business to buy from, work for and invest in. The "necessity" of being a responsible corporate entity on the planet has been made clear and is increasingly being adopted as a function of the enterprise. The next message is how to move, innovatively, from working separately on the parts to working with the whole. In the same way that mindfulness of the customer's need for quality should be imbedded in every act of the company, so must be CR. And the big jump will be how innovation is possible in CR and CR is possible in every innovation.

Brand Qualities: *Contrarian, Comprehensive, Consciousness producing—*

It is *contrarian* in that it challenges the sacred cows of best practices, sustainability as currently conceived, and stakeholders as only something to manage. It is *comprehensive, yet essentialized,* in that it integrates in a simple and straightforward way, everyone and every function in the enterprise, as well as every stakeholder to the aims of the enterprise. It is *Consciousness-producing* because it provides a way to order thinking, a consciousness infrastructure and language, which names and organizes experiences and thoughts people have had but had no way to articulate, comprehend or tackle.

3. **Product Offering: Consciousness Infrastructure for integrating and embedding CR in all business operations.** The pentad framework provides a systemic and systematic way to build innovation into CR work and to build CR into every aspect in a business. It builds greater consciousness by enabling business people to see and understand the interrelated effects of their decisions on all stakeholders (internal and external to the enterprise), and to deepen stakeholder relationships through time.

Roles of Buyers for this Book

1. Enterprise Wide and Business Unit managers
2. Managers who have aspirations to lead an enterprise with these values.
3. Leaders who have felt challenged to justify "people and sustainability" approaches to business improvement.
4. General Managers and Managing Directors of business units within an enterprise.
5. Training and development for building leadership and executive capability
6. Leaders of Educational Institutions from K-12 (Principles and Superintendents) through Graduate School (Academic and Administrative Deans) as well as managers in technical schools.
7. Government (State, Local National and International), and quasi government (Libraries and Utilities), leaders who often search for business practices.
8. Not-For-Profit Leadership who follow business trends
9. Urban and City planners
10. Economic Development executives
11. Faculty of University Business, Public Administration, Educational Administration for textbook assignments. E,g Rebecca Hendersen, Harvard Business School, Leadership and Corporate Accountability (she expressed interest) and Marshall Ganz,

Harvard Kennedy School, Leadership of Public Policy Discourse. A learning/field guy within six months and special materials such as additional research material on brain and behavior.

12. Libraries: Index and Case Studies make a good purchase.
13. Consultants in the fields of sustainability and corporate responsibility generally and trainers. A Field Book/learning guide will support consultants, trainers and faculty, approximately six months after publication of TRB.

Values of buyers: Leaders who value more than just the financials (Corporations who sell products, services, entertainment, sports) but are always searching for a more effective, even easier, more meaningful way to succeed and be corporately responsible as well. Such leaders place value on growing as people, as well as learning professionally and/or personally. They are driven by purpose, personal aims and missions as well as achievement of business goals; a commitment to a healthy planet and viable communities, healthy places to work and live, equity and justice for all people, diversity in ideas and opportunity, ecological health, spirit in the workplace, making a contribution that is unique and meaningful, including living systems (rivers, forests, habitats). They also believe the business world and organizations, with causes and missions—even government and quasi-government— are a place and means to do this. Those who believe the capitalistic system is a viable best means to do good will find a more effective way to achieve that as well. TRB readers also care about fair trade and the human condition everywhere on the planet. If they have children, they particularly care about what kind of future we are creating and what they can do about that.

Subject Interest of buyers: They fall into the category of those who seek new learning on social and environmentally responsibility, purpose focused, sustainability, innovation and learning processes, community involvement, green investing, supply chain sustainability, employee involvement, innovative work design, consciousness consumerism, local economics, small business, entrepreneurs in corporate responsibility product arenas, fair-trade, shareholder activism, steward leadership, non for profit organizations with social and environmental causes, green MBAs, young presidents, More traditional subjects will also be introduced in an innovative way because of the system and because of the unique presentation of the stakeholder potion and will attract buyers with interest in marketing and product design, human resource management, community development. And anyone interested in systems thinking and its application to organizations.

Complementary books: Pair well for promotion because someone who buys these will be interested in The Responsible Business

This book offers an extension to the following books:

1. *The Responsibility Revolution*, Jeffrey Hollender (Jossey Bass, Spring 2010) in how to carry out what he speaks is becoming the revolution. And how to do it systemically and systematically across the business. One chapter has extensive references to my work there and my contribution.

2. *Good to Great: Why Some Companies make the Leap . . . and Others Don't*, Jim Collins. Level Five leadership is difficult to understand. This book is based in processes that guide leaders who wish to be level five, including getting everyone "on the bus" to be Level Five leaders with ability to be "ruthlessly challenging" in a way that will not be taken personally. The system gives the means.

3. *The Fifth Discipline*, Peter Senge It takes systems thinking popularized by Senge, et. all, to systemic and systematic thinking, making it more accessible and meaningful. The systems thinking approaches in TRB are taken from living systems thinking instead of computer systems modeling. It also extends systems thinking into sustainability

4. *The Necessary Revolution*, Peter Senge. TRB brings back the idea of systems thinking which Senge first introduced to the world but with a significant upgrade and evolution to MIT models of Systems Thinking.

Pre-publication:
Set up web sites and blog sites: All linked

- ➤ Speakers website: Done *carolsanford.com*
- ➤ Company website: Done *Interoctave.com*
- ➤ Series Weblog and website: Done *wholeinonebook*.com
- ➤ *You tube channel Done: http://www.youtube.com/user/carolsanford2*
- ➤ Book website and Blog theresponsibleBusiness.com

BLOG Theme: Unveiling what is hidden, partial, incomplete and even destructive. What cannot be "seen" without critical thinking and reflection, comments on how using a whole approach to examine ideas, and proposed solutions. Commenting on practice and ethical view, and the effect on the nation and society if this approach is adopted full scale.

Sections of Blog— working from a Development View
The root of the word development is to remove the veil, "de-vel" in order to see what is hidden, especially in terms of potential.

Section One: **Exposed News**: Business, Education, or Not for Profit News Stories; commenting on what others have written or said in any media source; exposing the incompleteness of thought, where it exists, and showing what would make it more whole, or an alternative when more whole, particularly Harvard Business Review, MIT Sloan Review, and McKinsey Journal. Raises the rank in search engines.

Section Two: **Uncovered Books**: Digging into what Best Selling authors do NOT say in Business, Education or Not for Profit books; e.g. comment on what is missing, inaccurate and/or needs to add; how it fits with my book and ideas; duplicate use- place into review of books on Amazon and add the blog tag in it. Part of the contrarian and competitive arraction.

Section Three: **Bare Naked Practices;** Reveal the hidden downside of most Best Practices and what a leader can do to be whole rather than partial or damaging: introduce one idea a week for people to comment on that comes from my experience or a comment on best practices that are touted by others. Again, seeking to make other approaches more whole

Will be set up blogs so they are likely to get picked up by other blogs through RSS feeds and other such applications. Carol will input to other relevant blogs in order to attract attention to the whole business blog. I own the following domain names: **wholebusiness.net, wholebusiness.us.com, wholebusinesz.com**

➤ **Book Website will completed by December 2009:**

Sales link to Amazon associate routing and other book sellers. Capture sign up names to get articles for free. I own the following domain names: **WholeinOnethebook.com, whole-in-one.com, whole inone.us.com, theresponsibleBusiness.com**

Post Publication

Working with PR agent for appropriate posts. Including PRWebb.com

Send free articles to syndicators for posting, with my URL and link to booksellers:

- Amazon.com
- Bussle.com
- Ezinearticles.com
- IdeaMarketers.com

Book Reviews, including

- Executive Summary
- Book Reviews: On-Line all with Link to my Website URL and a connection to Amazon to buy immediately
- BookReview.com
- BookBrowse.com
- ComplusiveReader.com
- BookReporter.com
- BookIdeas.com
- BookPleasures.com
- BookLoons.com
- ReviewrChoice.com

- BookCrossing.com
- NewPages.com

Business Magazines: send book reviews and press releases with targeted material
- AmericaEconomia, *www.americaeconomia.com/*
- Business Week, *www.businessweek.com/*
- CEO Refresher, *www.refresher.com*
- Canadian Business, *www.canadianbusiness.com/*
- Chief Executive, *www.chiefexecutive.net/*
- Directors & Boards, *www.directorsandboards.com/*
- E:CO,
- Economist, *www.economist.com/*
- Entrepreneur, *www.entrepreneur.com/mag/*
- Fast Company, *www.fastcompany.com/*
- Forbes, *www.forbes.com/*
- Fortune *www.money.cnn.com/magazines/fortune/*
- Harvard Business Review, *www.hbsp.harvard.edu/* with Rebecca Hendersen
- INC, *www.inc.com/*
- International Journal of Business Performance Management, *www.inderscience.com/*
- Perdidomagazine, *www.perdidomagazine.com/*
- Strategy + business, *www.strategy-business.com*
- Newsweek | Smart Money | Time | US News |

Other Print Media:
- *Pink*-the magazine; trends effecting ambitious women
- ASAE catalogue, for Not For Profits; Association Leadership
- Live' Book Fairs, Speaking, buying booth space for promotion
- Imagine Nation Books- display marketing
  Daily News
  Boston Globe | Chicago Tribune | Christian Science Monitor | CNN | Los Angeles Times | New York Post | New York Times | Newsday | San Jose Mercury News | USA Today | Washington Post | BBC |

Globe and Mail | Herald Tribune | Le Monde | London Times | Wall Street Journal World Press Review/ Seattle Times

Business Knowledge and Schools
Universities: Speaking Engagements can be arranged (I have spoken at many of these and would be invited back
- Carnegie Mellon, Tepper School of Business,
- Columbia Business School,
- Cornell, The Johnson School,
- Dartmouth College, Tuck School of Business,
- Duke, Fuqua School of Business,
- Emory University, Goizueta Business School,
- Harvard Business School
- MIT, Sloan School of Management,
- New York U., Stern School of Business,
- Northwestern, Kellogg School of Management,
- Ohio State, Fisher College of Business,
- Purdue, Krannert School of Management,
- Stanford Graduate School of Business,
- U. Of California–Berkeley, Haas School of Business,
- UCLA, Anderson School of Management
- U. Of Chicago Graduate School of Business,
- U. Of Michigan, Ross School of Business,
- U. Of Pennsylvania, Wharton Business School Knowledge @ Wharton
- U. Of Virginia, Darden School of Business,
- Yale School of Management,

Radio/TV: Find targeted connections to talk radio/TV oriented for Business/psychological topics- examples of programs that match
- ABC, CBS, NBC news, CNN,
- Charlie Rose,
- Zohara Hieronimus with Future Talk and Clearview;
- Women Speak Out (controversial subjects;
- Leonard Lopate Show—Big Picture ideas;

- Lime Multi Platform Media: Good Company, The Business Shrink;
- Venture Talk Radio;
- Air American Radio; Small business Advocate;
- Focus 580;
- Greatness by Design;
- The Earth News Hour (Meria Heller);
- NPR *On Point*·
- After Words, CSPAN 2, Book coverage

Other Blogs: particularly for Book Reviews plus a story where appropriate

- 800CEOREAD, because I have international examples in the book
- Progressive on the Prairie
- Wallo World Blog
- Book Bloggers- Complete Review
- Agent 007 Publishing
- MJRose: Buzz, Balls, Hype
- Hot Psychology- business, growth change blog
- January Magazine
- Book Slut.com
- Bookninja- in depth culture reviews
- Jenny Davidson Light Reading *http://jennydavidson.blogspot.com/*
- The Elegant Variation
- Brandywine Books *http://www.brandywinebooks.net/*

Websites: for Book Reviews
- Human Nature Review *http://human-nature.com/feedback.htm*
- Booksonreview
- California Literary Review (Carol is an alumni from Cal Berkeley)
- Conversational Reading; Scott Esposito
- Books for Business *http://www.booksforbusiness.com/about.aspx*
- Amazon.com *Whole in One* will have the citations of the top 20 books of the last 5 years imbedded in it which causes the Amazon search engine to list it under- Better together, book reviews, listomania, "So you liked . . . " section; produced mini-video for site; Look-Inside

- WeLEAD, leadership education website *www.leadingtoday.org*
- Whole in One, the Book website; with Free reports and articles to attract connection, always mentioning a current topic in the media so it get picked up by search engines.
- Altar magazine- aksi website for social change

Conferences:
- Continue to speak at conferences and sell books at back of the room
- Sponsor at conference to get higher visibility
- Co-present with clients and professors to gain even higher level platform- I starting teaching at Harvard Business School as lecturer in Spring 2010 and co-publishing another book with Rebecca Henderson at HBS.

Membership I can leverage: Net Impact (Corporate Responsibility membership of students and professionals, as well as company memberships) Co-sponsor workshops, announcements and press materials with Net Impact (I am on the Board and they co-sponsor my work,

BALLE (Businesses for Local Economies) who announce my webinars regularly **Renaissance Weekend** which is an invitation only organization with has Presidents (e.g. Clinton, Ford, Royalty (Jordan's King and Queen mother), Journalists, CEO, Social Media Founders, Founders of Non-for profits, Professors, Librarians Faculty. The invitation requirement is to be a person who makes significant contributions and effects on the world. I was invited to join ten years ago. There are hundreds of prominent world figures at each of the 8 events each year and I attend at least one, someone more. Each of us are on 4-5 panels with our publications announced to t introduce us and are published in the attendance guide. With this book, I will be placed on panels of such subjects as listed for buyers and will have audiences that most people can only dream of being heard by. And I will speak once to the plenary event for 2-3 minutes. The person who brought Kathe Sweeney into the publishing world at Oxford press is a invited member, although he is not the one who introduced me to Kathe.

National Speakers Association—tables at conferences, websites, and subgroup memberships "meetings" are available to market as part of my membership

I am a member of the *Independent Book Publishers Association* and the *Small Publishers, Artists and Writers Network,* which has great resources for marketing and I have used effectively for digital materials.

Media Experience

Carol has extensive experience in Radio/TV and ability to generate interest in being covered.

- Cable Series on Strategic Leadership in Vancouver, WA, 3 years on business and family education subjects
- Small Business Adm. expert on Fox Cable for Northwest USA Region
- World Report, Public TV and radio, NPR

Carol has published over 100 works in 10 languages, including a column for "At Work", a newsletter with Berrett Kohler Press, and several pieces in Stephen Covey's newsletter, "Executive Excellence".

Star Hitching: *The Responsible Business* lends itself to current topics in the news (ethics in business, green) and human-interest stories where there is a message in the book beyond just business leaders (e. g. community development, non profits going green). The book can be hitched to other famous stories (Lehman Brothers type events, people such as Responsibility leaders, books, events and subjects; For example, corporate scandals, environmental problems or solutions, employee treatment and involvement, diversity, affirmative action, Sustainability etc.

News forums are always looking for alternative, contrasting, and contrary views. I am a rare voice who would not say "don't do green" but who could add a dimension that is never brought, opening up the interest for the news outlets. E. g. "we will not achieve our ends with sustainability practices because they are just cutting back on the harm we do. We cannot really do what matters until we learn to understanding how regeneration works. For example, what is the role of the piece on land in the watershed on which the building sits. The watershed cannot regenerate itself without our consciousness in how we support it". Most people say, "keep people out of things because they are the problem". I am a business voice which provides a way out of many CR dilemmas and not trading off conscience or cash flow.

Sample Pitch Letter

May 4, 2007
Name
Company
Address
City/State/Zip
Dear Name:

I'm sending you this press kit and review copy of *Live Your Road Trip Dream* at the request of Dan Parlow of MyTripJournal.com (GSC Personal Websites). Dan told me that you two had a nice conversation about me and our book this week, and I appreciate your willingness to take a look at it.

Why would you want to sell *Live Your Road Trip Dream*?

This book is timely

"When planning pleasure trips, RV prospects and owners agree the most important factors are visiting beautiful outdoor places, escaping daily pressures, . . . controlling budget and itinerary, and strengthening family relationships."—Lois Sumberg, VP of Research for Harris Interactive—the results of their 2001 survey Go RVing Communications Planning Study

- This how-to guide addresses these exact issues!
- There are lots of road trip/RV books—how-to, selecting an RV, "full-timing" and so on. But this book is about fulfilling your own dream trip of a lifetime and returning to your home with a lifetime of memories. It gets you going from the dreaming to the doing!

This book has a market and a marketing plan

Ten thousand Americans turn fifty every day, with over 45 percent of all adults wanting to travel within the United States (USA Today and a study by RVIA)

With 9.3 million Americans already on the road in RVs (RVIA), the market is exploding with people ready to travel and enjoy making their dream come true.

Boomers rank travel as a leading goal in retirement and predict their adventures will be their No. 1 expenditure. (From a Del Webb study)

- A well-thought-out marketing plan is being executed throughout the life of the book—print, electronic, internet and appearances all are included.
- The book won the 2006 Benjamin Franklin Award (Publisher's Marketing Assn.) for best marketed book.
- 2007 National Spokespeople—Recreation Vehicle Industry Assn. (RVIA)

It has been produced professionally and had excellent reviews

The book is friendly in tone, yet comprehensive in its detail.

—Marcella Gauthier, Escapees Magazine

. . . (they) thought of many things that others might forget when devising their own plans. The worksheets are excellent memory joggers.

—Janet Groene, Family Motor Coaching

(This book) is a practical and inspirational gift for RV owners, new retirees, or anyone who's ever dreamed of a cross-country expedition.

—Beth Harpaz, Travel Editor, Associated Press

- Over 100 media articles and reviews have praised the book
- Now in its third printing

- Produced using the highest professional standards of editing, design and production
- Finalist, ForeWord Magazine Book of the Year–Travel

I will check in with you in a couple of weeks to make sure you have received the book and to answer any questions you may have. Thank you for your consideration of *Live Your Road Trip Dream*. I look forward to working with you to add this title to your line-up of books catering to your Recreational Vehicle markets and customers.

Live Your Dreams
Carol White
President

Sample Extended Bio

Appropriate for a Program Director at a conference, club or organization.
Patricia Fry has been writing for publication since 1973, having contributed over a thousand articles to about 300 different magazines. She has 32 books to her credit, including *The Right Way to Write, Publish and Sell Your Book, How to Write a Successful Book Proposal in 8 Days or Less, The Successful Writer's Handbook, Promote Your Book, A Writer's Guide to Magazine Articles* and *The Author's Repair Kit*.

Her articles have appeared in *Writer's Digest Magazine, Entrepreneur, Woman's Life, Authorship, Freelance Writer's Report, Canadian Author, PMA Independent, Spannet, Writer's Journal, Cat Fancy, Your Health* and many, many others.

Patricia is the Executive Director of SPAWN (Small Publishers, Artists and Writers Network), a 15 -year-old networking organization for anyone interested in the publishing business. (*www.spawn.org*) She also writes the popular monthly *SPAWN Market Update*.

On behalf of SPAWN and her own publishing pursuits, she attends approximately half dozen book festivals each year and she's guest speaker/workshop leader at anywhere from 5 to 10 writing/publishing-related conferences and other events annually. Past venues include the Much Ado About Books event in Jacksonville, FL; a National Association of Women Writers (NAWW) conference in Arlington, TX; the St. Louis Writer's Guild Conference and Book Festival in St. Louis, MO (two consecutive years); the Pen Women Conference in Honolulu; the PNWA Conference in Seattle; the Wisconsin Regional Writers' Association Conference in Janesville, WI; Spring Book Show and Writers' Conference in Atlanta (two consecutive years); the San Diego State University Writers' Conference (several consecutive years) and several others throughout the U.S. She was the lead speaker at the SPAN Publishing Conference in 2006. And in May of that year, she was the first woman ever to be invited to give the keynote speech at a Toastmasters Convention in the Middle East. She spoke before 800 Toastmasters in Dubai.

While some of her books have been published by traditional publishers, Patricia established her own publishing company, Matilija Press, in 1983, before self-publishing was fashionable.

She is a full-time freelance writer and author and she also provides editorial services such as editing and ghostwriting as well as help writing book proposals, self-publishing and book promotion. Learn more about her books and services at *www.matilijapress.com*. Visit her informative publishing blog daily: *www.matilijapress.com/publishingblog*.

Speaking/Workshop topics include:
- Two Steps to Successful Publishing.
- How to Write a Killer Book Proposal.
- Publishing is Not an Extension of Your Writing.
- Book Promotion for the Bold and the Bashful.
- How to Get Your Book Reviewed Many Times Over.
- How to Promote Your Book Through Magazine Articles.
- The Anatomy of a Nonfiction Magazine Article.
- How to Break in to Magazine Article Writing.
- Platform-building Techniques and Tips.
  And many others.

Sample List of Ten Questions You Might Give an Interviewer

(For a book on family pet care.)

1: Tell us a little about your book and what compelled you to write it.

2: What is your background in this topic?

3: You filled one whole chapter on the benefits of sharing your home with a family pet—would you share some of your thoughts on this concept?

4: Your book has a rather unique flavor—would you elaborate on these unusual features?

5: What can the reader expect to gain or glean from this book? Why would they read it?

6: On page 79, you talk about how to involve children in caring for the family pet. Would you elaborate on that?

7: I understand you're doing some workshops—please describe your program—who is it for, what do you cover—where are they held?

8: Now you weren't a writer when you decided to write this book. Would you describe the process you went through to eventually produce it?

9: What would you suggest to others who are thinking about writing a book?

10: How can people get in touch with you—where can they purchase the book?

Sample Press Release 1: Announcing an event

FOR IMMEDIATE RELEASE

Contact: Name

Address

Phone

E-mail Address

DREAM OF THAT LONG VACATION? THEN MAKE IT HAPPEN!

Northwest authors Phil and Carol White will be at the Saratoga Springs Public Library at 49 Henry St. Saratoga Springs, on September 4th to share their travel tips, and the secrets to planning your own great travel adventure. You will learn what they gleaned from their yearlong odyssey around the United States. Their lively presentation and book signing will be held in the Community Room at 7 pm.

Where would your dream take you if you had a long time to just head out and travel? Would it be antiquing your way around the country, taking a sailboat trip around the world, visiting all the national parks, or maybe a trek through Asia suits your interests? The possibilities are endless.

While many people dream of taking that long trip of a lifetime, few actually make it happen. Oregonians Phil and Carol White really did "hit the road" for a whole year, while they still had their good health and sense of humor. They now speak to audiences encouraging them to head out on their own adventure of a lifetime.

Recently retired, the Whites decided that the time had come to live their road trip dream. All along the way, people peppered them with questions, not so much about what they were doing (everyone has their own dream), but about *how* they actually got out of town! It was with the encouragement of want-to-be travelers everywhere that their book, *Live Your Road Trip Dream* was created.

Whether your idea of that great adventure is a road trip or something else, the planning is much the same. The Whites, who are definitely upbeat about encouraging others to get moving from the "dreaming to the doing," laugh when describing the most often asked question: How to be with your travel companion on a 24/7 basis.

Phil provides a decidedly unabashed answer when he suggests, "You learn those two precious little words 'yes, dear' early on!" He continues on a more serious note adding, "You really learn to support each other on your off days, which you will both have. This is much easier than at home, because it is just the two of you with no outside influences to be considered. You really get to be two kids again, and it is great fun to share each day's adventures."

Join the Whites as they help you plan your own dream trip of a lifetime and "tour" their RV too if you so desire. To find out more about their adventures, go to their website at *www.roadtripdream.com*

Sample Press Release 2: Introducing a new book

For Immediate Release

Contact: Patricia Fry
Phone: xxx-xxx-xxxx

Creative Grandparenting Across the Miles
By Patricia L. Fry, $5.95, paperback, 70 pages

New Book Tells How to Establish a Relationship With Your Long-Distance Grandchildren

There are sixty million grandparents in the United States today, and a reported two-thirds of us have at least one grandchild who lives in another state. Distance doesn't impair the love we have for our grandchildren, nor does it dismiss our obligations as mentor, role model, teacher, historian, spiritual leader, support system, safety net, playmate and giver of unconditional love.

Many modern day grandparents, however, find it difficult to establish and maintain a relationship with their long-distance grandchildren, which is why author, Patricia Fry, wrote *Creative Grandparenting Across the Miles, Ideas for Sharing Love, Faith and Family Traditions.* This 70-page book holds a collection of ideas to help grandparents bond with their grandchildren and be an important influence in their lives despite geographic distance.

Included are:

- Tips for using the telephone more effectively with kids. For example, ensure conversations by being prepared; instead of relaying events, tell a story; leave the story unfinished so the child is eager for your next call or give telephone challenges.

- How to connect creatively through correspondence: Personalize your letters; keep memories alive through letters; become the family historian; make your letters educational and establish a common interest with the child.

- Ways to have fun with electronic communication.
- Great gift ideas for long-distance grandkids. Giving to grandchildren is one of a grandparent's greatest pleasures. Gift-giving is difficult, though, when the kids live away. This book shows grandparents how to work with the parents in choosing gifts and gives a dozen or so ideas for great gifts.
- Meaningful traditions that transcend the miles.
- Tips for being a good role model across the miles.

Today's grandparents face many hurdles, and this book is designed to help them develop a lasting bond with their grandchildren whether they live across the street of across the states.

Creative Grandparenting Across the Miles, Ideas for Sharing Love, Faith and Family Traditions, Ligouri Publications, *xxx-xxx-xxxx. www.xxx.xxxxxx.com*

Sample Tip Sheet

From Patricia Fry

Tips for a Successful Publishing Project

1: Study the publishing industry so you understand your options, the possible ramifications of your choices and your responsibility as a published author.

2: Define your purpose for writing this book. Make sure it is valid, not frivolous.

3: Determine your target audience. Who is most likely to read this book and how many people does this comprise?

4: Ascertain whether this book is needed/desired. Is there a market for this book?

5: Consider your platform—your following, your connections, your way of attracting readers. Why are you the person to write this book and who is going to care about reading it?

6: Create a marketing plan. How will you get word out about your book?

7: Find ways to build promotion into your book while you're writing it.

Patricia Fry is the author of 31 books, most of them related to writing and publishing. For much, much more on every aspect of this tips sheet, read Patricia Fry's book, The Right Way to Write, Publish and Sell Your Book. *http://www.matilijapress.com/rightway. html*

(This tip sheet comprises 130 words—perfect for, perhaps, newspapers, senior publications, authors' newsletters/magazines and so forth.)

Sample Author's Newsletter

Susan Daffron's National Association of Pet Rescue Professionals Newsletter designed to promote her organization and her book, *Funds to the Rescue: 101 Fundraising Ideas for Humane and Animal Rescue Groups*

July 15, 2010

NAPRP Newsletter

National Association of Pet Rescue Professionals

Welcome to all of our new members this week!

Recently, I received a question from a member asking how to go about getting sponsors for events and donations from businesses. She also wanted to know whether it's better to e-mail people or go in person.

I thought it was a good question, so I'm sharing my answer here too, since it may be something you are dealing with for upcoming fall fundraisers.

The main thing is that you have to ask ;-)

The best approach to getting donations is to always focus on what's in it for the business. What they want is the exposure. Supporting a charity makes THEM look good in the eyes of potential customers. Be sure to mention your sponsors in your advertisements, and make sure your sponsors know they'll be mentioned.

The big thing they are getting from associating with you is free advertising and PR. The best donation ideas are ones where they can donate something that would make a big difference to you, but doesn't cost them much out of pocket. A few thoughts are:

1. **Radio advertising.** The radio station has to pay the rent and salaries anyway. It doesn't cost them much to run another ad. Plus, in many cases, they have to run a certain amount of "public service ads."

2. **Restaurant coupons.** Again, it doesn't cost the biz much out of pocket, but a free meal is a big draw for things like raffles or auctions.

3. **Printing.** Many times you can get your flyers or products (like a calendar) printed up as a donation, particularly if you know of another company that's printing something at the same time. You can do what they call a "gang run" where your print job goes through the press at the same time as another. It costs the printer almost nothing except paper.

- 4. **Random products.** What's "trash" to one business may be treasure to you. Inventory that "isn't moving" can be another source of great raffle items. It can be cheaper for the business to donate an item to you than to continue to store it.

As for how to go about it, you might start with a letter or e-mail and then follow up by phone or in person. The best thing is face-to-face meetings. The larger the donation you are going after, the more personal "face time" you're probably going to have to put in.

Years ago, for a big fundraiser for an equine therapy organization, friends of mine walked down the main street of our tiny town and stopped into every single business. In one afternoon, they got an amazing amount of donations for a raffle and auction. It is possible, but it's work, and you have to deal with quite a lot of rejection too.

It's helpful to start with people you know personally. Try brainstorming with people in your organization and see who knows business owners. Make a list and start with people who know someone in your organization directly.

As always, thank you for all you do to help the animals!

~ Susan Daffron

Founder & President, NAPRP

Check Out the award-winning book *Funds to the Rescue: 101 Fundraising Ideas for Humane and Animal Rescue Groups*
Armed with the information in Funds to the Rescue, you'll never struggle for fund-raising ideas again. Click this link to learn more: *http://www.FundstotheRescue.com*
(Available in print, Kindle, and other e-book formats too!)

Choose from Two Membership Levels

If you're getting this newsletter, you are a free Helping Paw member of the National Association of Pet Rescue Professionals. Thank you for your commitment to helping animals! In addition to receiving this newsletter every week, you also receive call-in information for our monthly expert teleseminars, so you can listen live.

If you upgrade your membership to become a Golden Paw Insider, along with this newsletter and teleseminars, with your paid membership, you gain access to the private area of the NAPRP website. You can log in and access audio recordings of all teleseminars, grant information, worksheets, templates, articles you can customize, artwork, and a lot more (two hundred plus files and counting). You also receive a Member Spotlight page on our site and the opportunity to have your events listed on our blog. Read more about the benefits at *http://www.naprp.com*.

Get Your Pets on the Radio!

I do an online radio show (podcast) called *Take Me Home* for Pet Life Radio (*http://www.petliferadio.com*) that showcases adoptable pets in shelters and rescues. If you'd like to be a guest on my *Take Me Home* radio show and feature your animals, please contact me using our contact form at *http://www.naprp.com* (Click the Contact link on the right side; using the form ensures your message makes it past all our e-mail filters.) Visit the Take Me Home Show Contact Us

About Susan Daffron

Susan Daffron is the president and founder of the National Association of Pet Rescue Professionals. She is the president of Logical

Expressions, Inc., and the author of a number of books, including *Funds to the Rescue, Happy Hound, Happy Tabby, Publishize, Vegan Success, Web Business Success,* and four others which are published by LE. She has been doing writing and graphic design work since 1988 and been a shelter volunteer and vet tech. She has four dogs and two cats, all of whom were adopted from shelters and rescue groups.

You can "friend" Susan at Facebook or LinkedIn or follow her on Twitter.

About NAPRP

The National Association of Pet Rescue Professionals (NAPRP) is an organization dedicated to providing the tools and information rescue groups and humane organizations need to save more pet's lives. Members receive benefits in three areas: adopter education, fundraising and promotion, and administration and management.

Check out Susan Daffron's Books in the LE Store!

Read Back Issues of the NAPRP Newsletter on the Blog

Privacy: This newsletter is never sent without your permission. You are receiving this newsletter because you asked to get it. (Please see our privacy policy for more info.)

If you want to stop receiving the newsletter, please use the link at the bottom of the page and you will be removed automatically.

ABOUT THE AUTHOR

Patricia Fry is a career writer. She has contributed hundreds (maybe thousands) of articles to a variety of magazines and newsletters since 1973. Her articles have appeared in *Writer's Digest, Cat Fancy, Your Health, Entrepreneur Magazine, Los Angeles Times, The Artist's Magazine, Catholic Digest, Pages, The World and I, Western Horse, Canadian Author,* and many, many others. She is also the author of thirty-five books on subjects ranging from horses and cats, to local history and youth mentoring, to presenting a Hawaiian luau. In 1996, she penned a metaphysical memoir. Most of her books relate to writing and publishing.

Patricia is the executive director of SPAWN (Small Publishers, Artists and Writers Network), a networking organization and resource center established in 1996 for anyone who is interested in publishing. (*www.spawn.org*)

On behalf of SPAWN and her own publishing business (Matilija Press), she frequently conducts workshops and speaks before groups at writers' conferences and other venues throughout the United States. She has been in book promotion mode since A. S. Barnes published her first book in 1978.

Through this book, she shares over 250 of the best no- and low-cost book promotion ideas she has collected and perfected over the years.

INDEX

Books from Allworth Press

Allworth Press is an imprint of Skyhorse Publishing, Inc. Selected titles are listed below.

The Writer's Guide to Queries, Pitches and Proposals, Second Edition
by Moira Anderson Allen (6 x 9, 288 pages, paperback, $19.95)

The Author's Toolkit: A Step-by-Step Guide to Writing and Publishing Your Own Book, Third Edition
by Mary Embree (5 ½ x 8 ½, 224 pages, paperback, $19.95)

The Writer's Legal Guide: An Authors Guild Desk Reference
by Tad Crawford and Kay Murray (6 x 9, 320 pages, paperback, $19.95)

Business and Legal Forms for Authors and Self-Publishers, Third Edition
by Tad Crawford (8 3/8 x 10 7/8, 160 pages, paperback, $29.95)

The Complete Guide to Book Marketing, Revised Edition
by David Cole (6 x 9, 256 pages, paperback, $19.95)

The Complete Guide to Book Publicity, Second Edition
by Jodee Blanco (6 x 9, 304 pages, paperback, $19.95)

Marketing Strategies for Writers
by Michael Sedge (6 x 9, 224 pages, paperback, $24.95)

Successful Syndication: A Guide for Writers and Cartoonists
by Michael Sedge (6 x 9, 176 pages, paperback, $16.95)

Writing the Great American Romance Novel
by Catherine Lanigan (6 x 9, 224 pages, paperback, $19.95)

Making Crime Pay: An Author's Guide to Criminal Law, Evidence, and Procedure
by Andrea Campbell (6 x 9, 320 pages, paperback, $27.50)

The Birds and the Bees of Words: A Guide to the Most Common Errors in Usage, Spelling, and Grammar
by Mary Embree (5 ½ x 8 ½, 208 pages, paperback, $14.95)

The Perfect Screenplay: Writing It and Selling It
by Katherine Atwell Herbert (6 x 9, 224 pages, paperback, $16.95)

The Journalist's Craft: A Guide to Writing Better Stories
by Dennis Jackson and John Sweeney (6 x 9, 256 pages, paperback, $19.95)

To see our complete catalog or to order online, please visit *www.allworth.com*.